Introduction vii

Legal Disclaimer x

About The Author xii

Rome 1

    1. Skip the Colosseum Ticket Line 2

    2. Avoid Eating Near Major Landmarks 3

    3. Beware of Street Vendors and "Free" Souvenirs 4

    4. Don't Take Photos with Gladiators 6

    5. Skip the Trevi Fountain at Peak Hours 7

    6. Avoid Overpriced Gelato Shops 9

    7. Steer Clear of Pickpockets on Public Transportation 11

    8. Avoid Overpaying for Vatican Tours 12

    9. Avoid Currency Exchange Booths in Major Tourist Areas 14

    10. Skip Overhyped Souvenir Shops Near Landmarks 15

Venice 18

    1. Skip Gondola Rides in High Season 18

    2. Avoid Eating at Restaurants in Piazza San Marco 20

    3. Don't Feed the Pigeons 22

    4. Beware of Fake Murano Glass 23

    5. Avoid Staying in the City Center 24

    6. Avoid the Rialto Bridge at Peak Times 26

    7. Don't Buy Cheap Souvenirs from Street Vendors 28

    8. Avoid Using Water Taxis if You're on a Budget 29

    9. Steer Clear of Overpriced Gelato Stands 31

    10. Avoid Lugging Large Suitcases Through Venice's Narrow Streets 32

Florence 35

    1. Skip Market Vendors Selling Cheap Leather 36

2. Avoid Eating Near Piazza del Duomo 37

3. Steer Clear of Long Lines at the Uffizi Gallery 39

4. Don't Buy Souvenirs from Shops in Tourist Areas 41

5. Avoid Buying David Replicas from Street Vendors 42

6. Avoid Restaurants Offering "Tourist Menus" 44

7. Skip Visiting Piazzale Michelangelo at Midday 46

8. Avoid Buying Bottled Water at Tourist Spots 47

9. Don't Take Taxis Around the Historic Center 49

10. Avoid Buying Art from Unauthorized Street Artists 51

Milan 54

1. Avoid Shopping on Corso Vittorio Emanuele II for Cheap Fashion 55

2. Skip Dining Near the Duomo 56

3. Steer Clear of Tourist Souvenir Shops Near Major Landmarks 58

4. Avoid Taxi Rides for Short Distances 59

5. Don't Visit the Navigli District on Weekend Evenings 61

6. Skip Waiting in Line for Last Supper Tickets 62

7. Avoid Shopping in the Galleria Vittorio Emanuele II 64

8. Avoid Attending Fashion Week Without Planning 66

9. Don't Overpay for Aperitivo in the Trendy Zones 67

10. Skip Visiting Castello Sforzesco Midday 69

Naples 72

1. Avoid Driving in the City 72

2. Skip Tourist Restaurants Near Major Landmarks 74

3. Don't Take Unofficial Taxis 75

4. Avoid the Overcrowded Circumvesuviana Train at Peak Times 77

5. Don't Wander Alone at Night in Certain Areas 79

6. Avoid Eating Pizza Anywhere But Pizzerias 80

7. Don't Forget to Validate Your Train or Bus Ticket 82

8. Skip the Waterfront Souvenir Shops 83

9. Avoid Visiting Museums or Attractions on Sundays Without a Plan ... 85

10. Don't Neglect Personal Belongings in Crowded Areas 87

Verona 90

1. Avoid Visiting Juliet's Balcony at Peak Hours 90

2. Skip Dining Near Piazza delle Erbe 92

3. Don't Drive in the Historic Center 93

4. Avoid Taking a Gondola Ride on the Adige River 95

5. Skip the Juliet Statue Tradition 96

6. Don't Visit During the Opera Festival Without Planning 98

7. Avoid Overpriced Souvenirs Near Major Attractions 100

8. Don't Spend Too Much Time in Verona Without Exploring Nearby. 101

9. Avoid Buying Skip-the-Line Tickets from Unofficial Vendors 103

10. Don't Forget to Check the Opening Hours of Museums and Churches
.... 105

Bologna 107

1. Avoid Eating Near Piazza Maggiore 107

2. Don't Climb Both Towers 109

3. Avoid Visiting During the August Holiday 111

4. Don't Rely on Public Transportation for Short Distances 112

5. Avoid the Central Markets at Peak Hours 114

6. Skip Tourist Souvenir Shops Near the Two Towers 116

7. Don't Rush Through Bologna in a Day 117

8. Avoid Skipping the University District 119

9. Don't Miss Booking a Table at Popular Restaurants 120

10. Avoid Taxis and Opt for Biking 122

Pisa 125
1. Avoid Visiting the Leaning Tower at Peak Times 125
2. Skip the Overpriced Souvenir Stands Near the Tower 127
3. Don't Eat at Restaurants Near Piazza dei Miracoli 128
4. Avoid Staying in Pisa for a Whole Day 130
5. Skip Climbing the Tower if You're Claustrophobic 132
6. Avoid Visiting Pisa on Cruise Ship Days 133
7. Don't Forget to Explore Beyond the Tower 135
8. Avoid the Pickpockets in Crowded Areas 136
9. Don't Expect Pisa to Be Like Florence or Rome 138
10. Avoid Public Restrooms Near the Tower 139

Turin 142
1. Avoid Visiting Only the Shroud of Turin 142
2. Skip Dining in the Main Tourist Squares 144
3. Don't Ignore Turin's Aperitivo Culture 145
4. Avoid Rushing Through the Egyptian Museum 147
5. Don't Drive in the Historic Center 148
6. Don't Skip the Quadrilatero Romano District 150
7. Don't Skip a Visit to Mole Antonelliana 151
8. Avoid Visiting Only in Winter 153
9. Don't Miss the Palatine Towers 155
10. Avoid Underestimating Turin's Coffee Culture 156

Siena 159
1. Avoid Visiting During the Palio Without Proper Preparation 160
2. Skip Eating at Restaurants in Piazza del Campo 161
3. Avoid Climbing the Torre del Mangia at Midday 163
4. Don't Rely Solely on Public Transportation 164

5. Avoid Rushing Through the Siena Cathedral (Duomo) 166

6. Don't Miss Exploring Siena's Contrade Neighborhoods 167

7. Don't Visit Only for the Day 168

8. Avoid Missing a Visit to the Museo dell'Opera del Duomo 170

9. Don't Expect Siena to Be Like Florence 172

10. Avoid Overlooking Siena's Surrounding Countryside 173

Final Reflections 176

INTRODUCTION

Italy is one of the world's most captivating destinations, a place where history, culture, art, and stunning landscapes come together to create an unforgettable experience. From the ancient streets of **Rome** to the romantic canals of **Venice**, the Renaissance treasures of **Florence**, the elegant charm of **Turin**, and the medieval allure of **Siena**, Italy has something for every traveler. However, difficulties such as congested tourist spots, overpriced attractions, and occasionally disappointing experiences come along with its enormous popularity. This guide is intended to assist you in avoiding those typical blunders and maximizing your time in Italy.

This book isn't meant to change your plans or discourage you from visiting any of Italy's amazing locations. On the contrary, it's here to ensure that you get the **best** out of your travels by guiding you through the potential pitfalls. Italy's magic lies not only in its famous landmarks but also in its hidden gems, local experiences, and authentic moments. This guide will show you how to navigate through Italy's top cities, providing you with tips on what to avoid and how to uncover each destination's true essence.

We'll take you through the must-see cities and show you how to experience them without the frustration of long lines, overpriced meals, and tourist-heavy activities. In **Rome**, you'll learn how to bypass the crowded Colosseum queues and discover more intimate corners of the Eternal City. In **Venice**, we'll help you avoid the typical tourist traps like overpriced gondola rides, guiding you to more authentic experiences in this stunning lagoon city. We'll show you how to take advantage of **Florence**'s abundant artistic treasures without getting caught up in the crowds that congregate around the Duomo and important galleries.

We'll take you through **Turin**'s sophisticated aperitivo culture and its hidden gems, which are frequently missed by tourists. This will give you the opportunity to see a side of Italy that is frequently overlooked. You'll discover **Siena** beyond the famous **Piazza del Campo** and learn how to enjoy this medieval city's traditions without feeling rushed or overwhelmed. **Naples**, known for its chaotic energy and incredible food scene, requires a bit of insider knowledge to enjoy safely and smartly—this guide will ensure you navigate it well.

For those heading to **Milan**, we'll help you steer clear of the tourist-packed fashion districts and overpriced restaurants, leading you to the heart of the city's culture and charm. In **Bologna**, we'll show you how to avoid the tourist rush and dive into the city's rich culinary history, from its famous pasta to its vibrant markets. Additionally, we'll assist you in exploring Pisa's less well-known and more genuine gems by helping you see past the Leaning Tower.

The purpose of this guide is to empower you, not to demoralize you. It's important to view Italy more intelligently and thoughtfully rather than to avoid it. By learning what to skip, you'll have the time and space to enjoy what truly matters—the local culture, hidden neighborhoods, and unique experiences that make Italy so special. You'll find out how to travel through Italy without the frustration of overcrowded attractions, overpriced meals, and rushed itineraries. Instead, you'll have the freedom to savor the sights, sounds, and flavors of this remarkable country.

You'll walk the cobblestone streets of **Siena**, admire the breathtaking art of **Florence**, and enjoy a quiet aperitif in **Turin**—all with insider knowledge to avoid the common tourist traps. You'll discover the hidden treasures of Rome without getting lost in the crowds, and you'll experience Venice more like a local and less like a tourist.

In the end, this guide helps you customize your Italian experience, providing more than just advice on what not to do. You'll gain the tools to travel more deeply, experiencing Italy in a way that brings its history, culture, and beauty to life. Whether this is your first visit or your fifth, this book will help you travel smarter, ensuring that you make the most of every moment.

Prepare yourself to savor the finest of Italy. This guide will help you step off the beaten path, dodge the typical tourist frustrations, and immerse yourself in the true essence of one of the world's most beautiful and fascinating countries. **Buon Viaggio,** and here's to making your Italian adventure one to remember!

LEGAL DISCLAIMER

This guide's content is only meant to be used as general information, and readers are expected to understand that neither the publisher nor the author is offering financial, legal, or other professional advice. While every effort has been made to ensure that the information in this guide is accurate and current, the author and publisher make no representations or warranties regarding the accuracy, completeness, or currency of the information contained in this book.

Travel conditions, attractions, prices, and schedules are subject to change without notice, and the author and publisher cannot be held liable for any inconvenience, loss, injury, or damages incurred by readers as a result of using this guide. Before depending on any information for travel-related decisions, readers are urged to independently confirm it.

This guide is not intended to discourage travel to Italy or to any of the destinations mentioned. Instead, it is meant to provide helpful tips to enhance your travel experience by avoiding common tourist pitfalls. Individual travel experiences may differ, and the recommendations made are based on the opinions and experiences of the author.

The author and publisher are not responsible for the actions, safety, or behavior of travelers or any third parties mentioned in the guide, including but not limited to hotels, restaurants, attractions, or transportation services.

All content in this guide, including but not limited to text, images, and recommendations, is the intellectual property of the author and publisher. This guide may not be reproduced, distributed, or used for commercial purposes without permission.

By using this guide, you agree to hold harmless the author, publisher, and any affiliates from any claims, liabilities, or damages arising from your travel decisions based on the information contained herein.

Copyright © 2024 by Landon Mercer

All rights reserved.

No portion of this book may be reproduced in any form without written permission from the publisher or author, except as permitted by U.S. copyright law.

This publication is designed to provide accurate and authoritative information in regard to the subject matter covered. It is sold with the understanding that neither the author nor the publisher is engaged in rendering legal, investment, accounting or other professional services. While the publisher and author have used their best efforts in preparing this book, they make no representations or warranties with respect to the accuracy or completeness of the contents of this book and specifically disclaim any implied warranties of merchantability or fitness for a particular purpose. No warranty may be created or extended by sales representatives or written sales materials. The advice and strategies contained herein may not be suitable for your situation. You should consult with a professional when appropriate. Neither the publisher nor the author shall be liable for any loss of profit or any other commercial damages, including but not limited to special, incidental, consequential, personal, or other damages.

First edition 2024

ABOUT THE AUTHOR

Landon Mercer is a passionate traveler and author who has spent much of his life exploring the diverse cultures, landscapes, and histories of Europe. Born and raised in Romania, Landon developed a deep curiosity for the world around him at an early age. His passion for travel started with his solo trips across Eastern Europe, but his travels didn't take on a new significance or degree of discovery until he met **Emilia Mercer**, his future wife.

Emilia, a French native, shares Landon's enthusiasm for experiencing the world beyond the typical tourist routes. Together, they have explored countless European cities, towns, and hidden corners, always seeking the authentic heart of each place they visit. With Landon's Romanian ancestry and Emilia's French roots, they have a distinct viewpoint on Europe that enables them to navigate cultural quirks and gain a deeper understanding of each location.

Now in their mid-thirties, Landon (35) and Emilia (30) have made it their mission to help others travel smarter. Whether it's avoiding the overcrowded landmarks in Rome, discovering the quiet canals of Venice, or finding the best local wine in Tuscany, the Mercers believe that the best travel experiences come from thoughtful planning and a willingness to explore beyond the surface. Their philosophy of travel is to connect with the local culture and enjoy the journey rather than just crossing things off a list.

This book is the product of years of travel experience, countless road trips, and many nights spent under the stars in European cities and countryside alike. The Mercers have taken the time to distill their knowledge into a guide that helps travelers avoid common tourist traps and uncover the hidden treasures of each destination. They have shared useful advice and insider knowledge that only seasoned travelers can offer based on their own travel experiences throughout Europe.

Landon and Emilia have been motivated by the people they have met, the tales they have heard, and the customs they have encountered throughout their travels. This guide reflects their passion for authentic travel and their desire to help others experience the world with the same joy and curiosity. When they're not on the road, Landon and Emilia love spending time together, planning their next adventure, and sharing stories from their travels with friends and family.

With a shared passion for exploration and a deep love for Europe, Landon and Emilia hope this guide helps travelers see beyond the obvious, skip the common pitfalls, and create memories that will last a lifetime.

ROME

Rome, known as the Eternal City, is a place where ancient history and modern life collide. It's a city that evokes awe with its majestic ruins, timeless art, and rich culture. From the Colosseum to the Vatican, the landmarks of Rome are some of the most recognized and visited in the world. Rome's history spans more than two millennia, so it should come as no surprise that millions of tourists visit each year, eager to walk the same streets that pope, emperors, and artists once walked.

However, with its popularity comes the inevitable downside: crowded attractions, long lines, overpriced restaurants, and the occasional scam targeting unsuspecting tourists. Many visitors discover that they are spending more time battling crowds or standing in line than actually taking in the wonders of the city.

This guide aims to save you from those typical mistakes and show you the Rome that lies just below the surface of the tourist traps. Whether it's skipping the Colosseum line, avoiding overpriced gelato, or knowing where to find authentic Roman cuisine away from the crowds, you'll be equipped to experience Rome like a savvy traveler.

Though the Eternal City has a wealth of history, you don't have to spend your time in long queues or excessively paying for tainted experiences. By following the tips and advice in this guide, you'll be able to explore Rome with more ease and discover its true magic—without falling for the common tourist traps. After all, Rome is meant to be savored, not rushed.

1. SKIP THE COLOSSEUM TICKET LINE

When visiting Rome, one must make time to see the Colosseum. This ancient amphitheater, which was built nearly 2,000 years ago, is one of the most iconic landmarks in the world. However, while the Colosseum is undoubtedly a bucket-list destination, the ticket lines can turn your visit into a frustrating ordeal.

WHY SKIP THE LINE?

The Colosseum attracts millions of visitors yearly, and the ticket lines can stretch for hours, especially during peak seasons. Waiting in line under the hot Roman sun can waste valuable time that could be spent exploring the city's other treasures. It is a tiring experience to walk around the Colosseum because of the overwhelming number of tourists, street sellers, and people.

WHAT TO DO INSTEAD?

- **Buy Tickets Online in Advance:** Purchase tickets from the official Colosseum website and select a timed-entry slot. This makes the process seamless and enables you to bypass the general admission line.
- **Purchase a Combination Ticket:** Opt for a ticket that includes the Roman Forum and Palatine Hill. Long lines at the Colosseum can be avoided by purchasing this combo online or at the Forum entrance.
- **Join a Skip-the-Line Tour:** Guided tours come with skip-the-line privileges and often include exclusive access to limited spaces like the underground chambers or arena floor.
- **Use a Roma Pass or Omnia Card:** These city passes provide skip-the-line access to the Colosseum and other major attractions. They are a convenient option since they also provide free public transportation.
- **Visit During Off-Peak Hours:** To avoid crowds, visit early in the morning or late in the afternoon. This lets you enjoy the Colosseum with fewer people and in chilly weather.

ADDITIONAL TIPS:

- **Stay Hydrated:** Rome experiences extreme heat, so bring water and sunscreen to stay comfortable during your visit.
- **Wear Comfortable Shoes:** The terrain is uneven around the Colosseum, Roman Forum, and Palatine Hill, thus, comfy shoes are essential.

By making advance plans, you can skip the ticket lines and make the most of your time at the Colosseum. Maximize your visit by exploring the ancient history without the hassle of long waits, leaving you more time to enjoy the wonders of Rome.

2. AVOID EATING NEAR MAJOR LANDMARKS

Rome's landmarks—like the Colosseum, Vatican, and Pantheon—are must-see attractions, but the restaurants nearby are often overpriced and underwhelming. It could seem sensible to have a quick meal close to these locations, but you'll usually end up paying a premium for low-quality food designed to cater to tourists.

WHY SHOULD YOU AVOID IT?

The restaurants around major landmarks in Rome are notorious for offering mediocre food at inflated prices. A basic pasta dish close to the Colosseum could cost two or three times as much as one located a few blocks away. These spots rely on a constant flow of tourists, so they have little incentive to provide authentic Italian dishes or quality service. Instead, you'll often find bland, "tourist-friendly" versions of Roman classics.

Dining near landmarks also means dealing with crowds and rushed service. These eateries put a higher priority on quick service than providing the relaxed dining atmosphere that Italians are renowned for, which can make your meal feel cold and unfulfilling.

WHAT TO DO INSTEAD?

- **Venture a Few Streets Away:** Step out from the main attractions and take a quick stroll. Rome is full of hidden gems just off the beaten path, where you'll find better food at more reasonable prices. Local trattorias just a few blocks from tourist sites often serve traditional Roman dishes made with fresh ingredients.

- **Look for Family-Owned Restaurants:** Step out from the main attractions and take a quick stroll. Here, you'll find classic Roman meals like cacao e pepe and carbonara prepared with care. These places are more likely to serve local customers and provide a genuine taste of Italy.
- **Eat Like a Local:** Italians dine later than tourists—Usually, lunch is between 1 PM and 2:30 PM, and dinner doesn't start until after 7 PM. Following local dining hours will help you avoid heavy tourists spots and discover places where Romans eat.
- **Don't Be Tempted by the View:** Restaurants with great views of attractions like the Trevi Fountain may look appealing, but the food rarely lives up to the scenery. Capture images of the landmark with your camera, then find a better place to eat a few streets away.

ADDITIONAL TIPS

- **Check Menu Prices Before Sitting:** Restaurants near milestones often charge inflated prices for simple dishes. Check the menu before committing to avoid a costly meal.
- **Beware of Hidden Cover Charges:** Some restaurants near tourist areas add extra service fees, so always enquire in advance about any additional costs.

You'll save money and enjoy better food and a more genuine dining experience if you steer clear of these tourist traps. Exploring Rome's culinary scene should be as enjoyable as its historical landmarks—so take the time to find meals that match the city's timeless charm.

3. BEWARE OF STREET VENDORS AND "FREE" SOUVENIRS

As you wander through the bustling streets of Rome, especially near famous landmarks like the Colosseum, Vatican, or Spanish Steps, you'll likely encounter street vendors offering "free" bracelets, flowers, or small trinkets. These presents could initially appear to be a kind gesture or an innocuous memento, but in actuality, they are frequently a part of a scam meant to deceive travelers.

WHY SHOULD YOU AVOID IT?

Street vendors will often approach tourists with a "gift" in hand, placing a bracelet on your wrist or handing you a flower with a smile. Once you accept it, they'll follow up by demanding money, often in an aggressive or guilt-inducing manner. Some people might say they gave you the item for free but then put pressure on you to pay, making what could have been a nice gesture into a tense exchange.

Many times, tourists feel pressured to pay without realizing they've fallen victim to fraud. This can lead to paying far more than the item's actual value. Worse still, these interactions can leave you feeling harassed, especially if the vendors become persistent or refuse to leave you alone after you decline.

WHAT TO DO INSTEAD?

- **Politely Decline:** Declining politely right away is the best way to steer clear of these situations. If someone approaches you with a bracelet or flower, simply say "No, thank you" and walk away. Don't feel pressured to accept anything, even if it's presented as a gift.
- **Be Aware of Your Surroundings:** Street vendors are frequently found in congested areas close to well-known landmarks. Be mindful of your surroundings and avoid engaging with anyone who approaches you too closely or insists on giving you something for "free."
- **Don't Feel Obligated:** You should not feel pressured to pay for an item you unintentionally take. Return it immediately, and if they persist, stand your ground and walk away. The vendors rely on tourists feeling guilty or uncomfortable, but you are under no obligation to pay for something you didn't ask for.
- **Avoid Crowded Tourist Spots During Peak Hours:** If possible, visit

major landmarks early in the morning or later in the evening when there are fewer street vendors and crowds. By doing this, you may lessen the likelihood of encountering pushy sellers.

ADDITIONAL TIPS

- **Watch Your Belongings**: While some vendors are simply trying to sell trinkets, others may be working with pickpockets. Take care and make sure your possessions are safe, especially in crowded places.
- **Stick to Official Souvenir Shops**: If you'd like a souvenir from your journey, buy from official stores or local markets where prices are clear and the shopping experience is more enjoyable.

You can enjoy your time in Rome hassle-free by avoiding the street vendor trap and being aware of these common strategies. These "gifts" are rarely free, and it's better to politely decline than to deal with the pressure and discomfort that comes afterward. Stay alert, and you'll have a more peaceful and pleasant experience exploring the city.

4. DON'T TAKE PHOTOS WITH GLADIATORS

Near the Colosseum and other famous Roman landmarks, you'll often see people dressed as gladiators offering to pose for photos with tourists. This can quickly turn into an uncomfortable and expensive situation, even though it might seem like a unique and enjoyable souvenir.

WHY SHOULD YOU AVOID IT?

The cost of taking a photo with these costumed gladiators is often not mentioned upfront, and after the picture is taken, they can demand as much as €20 or more. They might get combative if you try to offer less or refuse to pay. This turns what was supposed to be a lighthearted moment into a stressful encounter.

Moreover, these performers are not officially licensed, and the practice is often targeted by local authorities. In some cases, the police may step in, which could create an awkward or even tense situation for tourists caught in the middle.

WHAT TO DO INSTEAD?

- **Politely Decline:** Simply saying "no, thank you" and turning away is the best way to avoid this situation. Don't feel pressured to take a photo, even if they seem friendly or persistent. Most will move on quickly if you show no interest.
- **Take Your Own Photos:** You don't need a posed photo with a gladiator to capture your memories of Rome. Take your own pictures of iconic landmarks like the Colosseum, which will be more meaningful and come without the extra hassle.
- **Be Aware of Quick Posing:** Occasionally, the gladiators may attempt to force you into a pose or attempt to rapidly place props in your hands. Stay alert and avoid letting them rush you into a situation where you feel obligated to pay.
- **Choose Authentic Experiences:** For a more genuine experience, consider a guided tour of the Colosseum, which often includes access to special areas like the underground chambers. Compared to an expensive photo op with a street performer, these tours are far more rewarding and provide historical context.

ADDITIONAL TIPS

- **Set Boundaries**: If you decide to take a photo, always agree on a price upfront to avoid surprises.
- **Support Local Artisans**: Instead of spending money on staged photos, buy authentic souvenirs from local markets.

By avoiding these street performers, you'll save money and steer clear of unnecessary tension during your Roman adventure.

5. SKIP THE TREVI FOUNTAIN AT PEAK HOURS

One of Rome's most well-known and stunning landmarks, the Trevi Fountain draws tourists from all over the world. Tossing a coin into the fountain is a tradition that is said to ensure your return to Rome. However, visiting the Trevi Fountain during peak hours can be a frustrating experience due to massive crowds that detract from its beauty.

WHY SHOULD YOU AVOID IT?

At peak times—usually between late morning and late afternoon—the area around the Trevi Fountain is packed with tourists, making it difficult to move, take photos, or even enjoy the fountain's grandeur. You'll find yourself shoulder-to-shoulder with others, fighting for a spot to toss your coin or capture a quick selfie. What could be a magical moment can be ruined by the crowded atmosphere.

The fountain area is also a hotspot for pickpockets due to the large number of distracted visitors. Tourists often focus on taking photos or finding a good spot by the fountain, making them simple pickings for criminals.

WHAT TO DO INSTEAD?

- **Visit Early in the Morning or Late at Night:** To avoid the crowds, plan your visit early in the morning, ideally before 8 AM, or late at night after 9 PM. You can take in the tranquil atmosphere of the fountain during these slower hours. The early morning light or the soft evening glow adds a special charm to the experience, and you'll have a better chance of getting that perfect photo without the crowds.
- **Consider a Night Visit:** The Trevi Fountain is beautifully lit up at night, making it a great option for a romantic or peaceful visit after the daytime rush has died down. You'll have more room and a better view during these hours because fewer people hang out in the area.
- **Plan for a Short Stop:** If you can't visit at any time of day due to scheduling conflicts, consider making a quick stop during the day. Take a quick photo and enjoy the view from a distance, then move on to less crowded parts of the city.

ADDITIONAL TIPS

- •Hold Onto Your Belongings: Stay aware of your surroundings, as pickpockets are common in crowded areas like the Trevi Fountain.
- •Toss the Coin with Your Right Hand: According to tradition, you should toss a coin over your left shoulder with your right hand to ensure a return to Rome.

By visiting the Trevi Fountain at off-peak times, you'll avoid the crowds and enjoy a much more tranquil experience of this iconic Roman landmark.

6. AVOID OVERPRICED GELATO SHOPS

One of the most typical Italian sweets is gelato, and Rome is dotted with gelaterias serving up this rich, creamy treat. However, not all gelato is created equal, and many of the shops located near major tourist attractions charge outrageous prices for low-quality, mass-produced gelato. Knowing how to spot the tourist traps can save you from paying too much for a subpar experience.

WHY SHOULD YOU AVOID IT?

Tourist-oriented gelato shops can be found close to well-known sites like the Spanish Steps, Trevi Fountain, and the Colosseum. These places often charge inflated prices—sometimes upwards of €10 for a single cone—and the quality is rarely worth the cost. The gelato in these touristy spots is often mass-produced, overly sweet, and loaded with artificial colors and flavors to appeal to visitors rather than offer an authentic Italian experience.

Furthermore, a few of these gelaterias exploit visitors by hiding prices or charging more for "extras" like cones or whipped cream. Visitors are often surprised by the high price after ordering, turning what should be a delightful treat into an expensive mistake.

WHAT TO DO INSTEAD?

- **Look for Natural Colors:** Authentic, high-quality gelato is made with natural ingredients, and its colors should reflect that. Avoid gelato that looks unnaturally bright or neon-colored. Banana gelato, for instance, ought to be a soft yellow color rather than an intense one. The higher the quality, the more natural the color.

- **Find Gelato Stored in Metal Tins:** Genuine gelato is often stored in metal tins with lids, which help preserve the texture and freshness. If you see gelato piled high in plastic tubs, it's likely mass-produced and filled with additives to make it look more appealing.
- **Venture Away from Tourist Spots:** As with many things in Rome, the best gelato is found a few streets away from major tourist attractions. Take a short walk and look for smaller, family-owned gelaterias, where locals go for their daily fix. These establishments are more likely to provide affordable, real, handmade gelato.
- **Check the Price List:** To prevent surprises, always review the price list before placing an order. A good gelateria will have clearly displayed prices for different sizes and options. Be wary of places that don't show prices upfront, as they may be trying to take advantage of tourists.

ADDITIONAL TIPS

- •**Choose Seasonal Flavors**: In true gelaterias, flavors are frequently changed according to what's in season. Look for flavors like pistachio, hazelnut, or fresh fruit, which are typically made from real ingredients.
- •**Avoid Gelato Shops with Giant Displays**: Shops with huge, towering displays of gelato are often trying to lure in tourists with aesthetics rather than quality.

By seeking out authentic gelaterias away from tourist hubs, you'll enjoy a true taste of Italian gelato without overpaying. Making the extra effort to locate the ideal location will result in a much more delightful and fulfilling experience.

7. STEER CLEAR OF PICKPOCKETS ON PUBLIC TRANSPORTATION

Rome's public transportation system—especially its buses and metro—offers a convenient and affordable way to get around the city. But it's also a magnet for pickpockets, just like a lot of popular tourist spots.

Crowded buses and metro stations provide the perfect environment for thieves who prey on distracted travelers. You can prevent yourself from becoming a victim by learning self-defense techniques.

Pickpockets often operate on popular bus routes, like the ones heading to the Colosseum or Vatican, and in busy metro stations such as Termini. They take advantage of crowded spaces where tourists are focused on their destination, leaving bags and pockets vulnerable. These burglars are adept at working swiftly and stealthily; they frequently take valuables like phones, wallets, and passports without the victim realizing it until it's too late.

Tourists are prime targets because they often carry valuable items and may not be as familiar with the city's environment. Losing personal belongings in a foreign country can disrupt your trip and cause unnecessary stress.

WHAT TO DO INSTEAD?

- **Keep Your Belongings Secure:** Always be mindful of where you keep your valuables. Use a secure, zippered bag or a money belt worn under your clothing to store important items like your wallet, phone, and passport. Since your back pockets are common places for pickpockets to target, avoid carrying anything valuable in them.
- **Stay Alert in Crowded Areas:** Pickpockets thrive in busy, crowded environments. Be especially cautious when using public transportation during peak hours or when entering and exiting metro stations. In crowded areas, keep your bag in front of you and hold it close to your body.
- **Avoid Flashing Valuables:** Try not to draw attention to your priceless

possessions. Don't pull out large sums of money, expensive cameras, or other electronics in crowded areas. Keeping a low profile can reduce the chances of being targeted by pickpockets.
- **Use Anti-Theft Bags:** Think about utilizing bags made especially to deter theft. These bags often feature hidden zippers, cut-resistant straps, and compartments that make it difficult for pickpockets to access your belongings.
- **Take Taxis or Walk in Less Crowded Areas:** If public transportation feels too risky or is too crowded, consider walking or taking a licensed taxi for short distances. This can assist you in avoiding dangerous locations such as packed buses and metro stations.

ADDITIONAL TIPS

- **Beware of Distractions:** Some pickpockets work in teams, where one person creates a distraction (like dropping something or asking for help) while another steals your belongings. Remain concentrated, particularly in crowded spaces.
- **Keep a Copy of Important Documents:** In case your passport or other valuable documents are stolen, always keep a digital or photocopy of them in a safe place. This will facilitate their replacement should the need arise.

By staying alert and taking simple precautions, you can significantly reduce the risk of being pickpocketed while using public transportation in Rome. You can visit the city worry-free and travel with peace of mind if your possessions are safe.

8. AVOID OVERPAYING FOR VATICAN TOURS

One of the highlights of any trip to Rome is seeing the Vatican, but it's also one of the places where guided tour prices can easily go up for visitors. Many unofficial tour operators and street vendors offer "exclusive" access or special tours, often at inflated prices. These offers can be tempting, but they're rarely worth the extra cost.

WHY SHOULD YOU AVOID IT?

Street vendors near the Vatican often approach tourists with promises of fast-track access to skip the long lines or exclusive entry to parts of the Vatican not available to the general public. These trips are frequently overpriced, sometimes costing up to €50 for an experience that could be had for much less money. Worse, the quality of the tours can be poor, with guides rushing through explanations or providing minimal historical context.

In many cases, the Vatican Museums and St. Peter's Basilica already offer easy options for skipping the line with advance online bookings or official guided tours, making the offers from street vendors unnecessary and expensive.

WHAT TO DO INSTEAD?

- **Book Tickets Online:** You can purchase timed-entry tickets through the official online booking system of the Vatican Museums. This guarantees you'll skip the general admission line without the need to pay extra for a tour you don't want. Booking in advance is the easiest way to ensure a smooth visit.
- **Use Official Vatican Guides:** Direct reservations for guided tours can be made via the Vatican's official website. These tours are well-organized, informative, and far less likely to rush you through the experience. You'll also know exactly what you're paying for and avoid hidden costs.
- **Arrive Early or Visit Late:** If you don't want to book in advance, visiting early in the morning or later in the afternoon can help you avoid the worst of the crowds. St. Peter's Basilica opens early, and arriving right at the opening can often mean little to no wait time.

ADDITIONAL TIPS

- **Ignore Street Vendors:** Politely decline offers from street vendors claiming to sell special Vatican tours. Stick to official ticket outlets.
- **Explore the Vatican Gardens:** For a unique experience, consider a tour of the Vatican Gardens, which can be booked directly through the Vatican Museums' website.

By booking your Vatican visit through official channels, you'll save money and avoid the hassle of dealing with overpriced and low-quality tours. Take in the Vatican's splendor and legacy without spending more than is necessary.

9. AVOID CURRENCY EXCHANGE BOOTHS IN MAJOR TOURIST AREAS

When traveling to Rome, you may find yourself needing to exchange currency, but using exchange booths in tourist-heavy areas like near the Vatican, Spanish Steps, or Termini Station can end up costing you far more than expected. To entice tourists, these booths frequently offer "no commission" or "special rates," but the true cost is concealed by the unfavorable exchange rates.

WHY SHOULD YOU AVOID IT?

When compared to other methods, currency exchange booths near major attractions often offer poor exchange rates. Even if they claim to have "no commission," the rate they use for converting your money is often much lower than the official rate, meaning you'll lose out on more money than expected. In addition, some booths add hidden fees or charges that aren't clear upfront.

Many travelers also feel rushed or confused by the language barrier and end up accepting poor deals without fully understanding the cost. This has the potential to make a straightforward transaction costly.

WHAT TO DO INSTEAD?

- **Use ATMs:** Using an ATM is the simplest and most economical way to obtain local currency. ATMs typically offer much better exchange rates than currency exchange booths, and withdrawing directly from your bank account often means you'll only pay a small foreign transaction fee, which is much lower than the costs associated with exchange booths.
- **Bring a Travel-Friendly Credit or Debit Card:** Credit or debit cards with no foreign transaction fees are provided by certain banks, which makes them perfect for traveling abroad. Using these cards to withdraw cash or

make purchases directly can save you money compared to exchanging cash.
- **Exchange Currency Before You Travel:** If you would rather have cash with you when you get there, exchange a small amount at your local bank before you leave. This way, you'll avoid the inflated rates at airport or tourist-area booths and can have local currency ready for immediate expenses like transportation or snacks.

ADDITIONAL TIPS

- **Check Exchange Rates Online**: Prior to making any money exchanges, check the current exchange rate online so you know what to expect.
- **Avoid Airport Exchange Booths**: Exchange rates at airports are typically just as bad as those in tourist areas. Plan ahead to avoid paying more than necessary.

By avoiding currency exchange booths in tourist areas and sticking to ATMs or travel-friendly cards, you'll save yourself from unfavorable rates and hidden fees, leaving extra cash to fully enjoy your stay in Rome.

10. SKIP OVERHYPED SOUVENIR SHOPS NEAR LANDMARKS

While visiting Rome, it's natural to want to take home a piece of the city's charm in the form of souvenirs. However, the souvenir shops clustered around significant attractions like the Colosseum, Vatican, and Trevi Fountain are often overpriced and filled with low-quality, mass-produced items. These shops are always busy with tourists, but the things they sell don't really show off Italy's heritage and craftsmanship.

WHY SHOULD YOU AVOID IT?

The shops near famous landmarks are notorious for inflating prices, knowing that tourists are likely to make impulse purchases. A little item, such as a keychain or a Colosseum replica, might cost twice or three times as much as it would elsewhere. Moreover, many of these items are cheaply made, often imported, and lack the authentic touch of local craftsmanship that makes Italian souvenirs special.

In addition, these shops may pressure tourists into buying items they don't really want or need, especially if they sense you're in a hurry or unsure of your choices. If poor quality and expensive prices are combined, you might receive a memento that is disappointing.

WHAT TO DO INSTEAD?

- **Explore Local Markets:** For a more authentic and reasonably priced souvenir, explore local markets like **Campo de' Fiori or Mercato Monti**. These markets offer a variety of goods, from handmade crafts to vintage items, all while supporting local artisans and businesses.
- **Look for Artisan Shops:** Rome is home to many small, family-owned shops where you can find handcrafted goods, such as leather products, jewelry, or ceramics. These items are often made by local artisans using traditional methods, offering a far more meaningful and high-quality memento.
- **Buy Specialty Food Items:** Since Italy is renowned for its cuisine, think about packing eatable trinkets like pasta, wine, or olive oil. Visit small grocery stores or food markets for authentic local products that you can enjoy long after your trip.

ADDITIONAL TIPS

- **Check for Authenticity:** Look for items marked "Made in Italy" to ensure you're buying something genuinely local rather than a mass-produced product.
- **Avoid Last-Minute Shopping:** Don't wait until you're right next to a major landmark to buy souvenirs. Plan your shopping earlier in the trip at more authentic locations.

You can save costs and bring home more thoughtful and beautifully made mementos by avoiding the tourist trap souvenir shops around Rome's famous sites. Exploring local markets and artisan shops will provide you with unique treasures that reflect the true spirit of Rome.

Rome, also known as the Eternal City, is incredibly rich in culture, history, and natural beauty. However, as one of the world's most visited cities, it's also full of tourist traps that can take away from the authenticity of your experience. By knowing what to avoid—whether it's long lines, overpriced restaurants, or street vendors selling "free" souvenirs—you can make the most of your time and immerse yourself in the true essence of Rome.

Rome's true charm is found in its smaller lanes, neighborhood trattorias, undiscovered ruins, and off-the-beaten-path exploration opportunities. With a little planning and attention to detail, you can explore Rome like a seasoned traveler, enjoying its rich history and vibrant culture without the crowds and inflated prices.

With this guide, you can make the most of every moment in Rome, from visiting historical sites to enjoying the best local cuisine. In Rome, there's always something new to discover, and with these tips, you'll experience the city in a way that's both memorable and genuinely Roman.

VENICE

Venice, one of the most charming cities in the world, is known for its romantic gondolas, winding canals, and centuries-old architecture. Known as "La Serenissima," this floating city captures the imagination of travelers with its unique beauty and rich history. However, as one of the most popular tourist destinations on the planet, Venice also comes with its fair share of challenges.

From overpriced gondola rides to overcrowded squares and hidden tourist traps, navigating Venice can be overwhelming for first-time visitors. The best way to appreciate Venice's charm is to know how to avoid the typical pitfalls that could make your trip less enjoyable.

With the aid of this guide, you can avoid the tourist traps, save costs, and discover Venice's true nature. Whether it's avoiding the crowds at the Rialto Bridge, steering clear of expensive gelato, or knowing the best ways to enjoy the canals, you'll find practical tips here to make the most of your Venetian adventure. With a little insider information, you can explore this enchanted city and avoid falling victim to the typical tourist traps. Venice has a lot to offer.

1. SKIP GONDOLA RIDES IN HIGH SEASON

Although many people think that taking a gondola ride along Venice's picturesque canals is an absolute must for visitors, this famous experience may not always be as enjoyable as one might hope during the busiest travel times. While the romantic image of gliding through the canals on a gondola is what draws many visitors, high prices and crowded waterways can detract from the magic.

WHY SHOULD YOU AVOID IT?

The canals are crammed with other gondolas during peak season, particularly in the summer, which makes the ride feel more like a traffic jam than a tranquil experience. Gondoliers may rush through the journey to accommodate the long lines of tourists waiting for their turn, which can diminish the charm of the ride.

Prices are also at their highest during the busy season. Gondola rides in Venice are already pricey—typically around €80 for a 30-minute ride during the day and even more for evening rides. Gondoliers may charge even more during busy times of the year, so you'll be paying top dollar for a packed, rowdy ride.

WHAT TO DO INSTEAD?

- **Take a Vaporetto (Water Bus):** Venice's public water buses, known as vaporetti, offer a more affordable way to enjoy the city's waterways. For the price of a standard ticket (about €7.50), you can hop on a vaporetto and enjoy a scenic trip along the Grand Canal, passing many of Venice's famous sights. Even though it's not as private as a gondola, this is still a fantastic way to take in Venice's splendor without having to pay a high price.
- **Try a Traghetto:** If you want a brief gondola experience, consider taking a **traghetto**. At specific points, these shared gondolas traverse the Grand Canal. A ride on a traghetto costs only about €2, and though the ride is short, you'll still get the authentic gondola feel without the high cost.
- **Visit During the Off-Season:** If you've always wanted to take a gondola ride, you should go to Venice between November and February, which is the off-season. The crowds are much smaller, and you're more likely to get a peaceful, scenic ride without the chaos of high-season traffic. Plus, prices may be more reasonable during these quieter months.

ADDITIONAL TIPS

- **Negotiate the Price**: If you still want to take a gondola ride in peak season, try negotiating the price with the gondolier before the ride begins. Even though prices are normally fixed, if business is slow, some gondoliers might be open to making a better offer.

- **Evening Rides Are More Expensive**: Gondola rides after 7 PM cost significantly more than daytime rides. If you're on a budget, opt for a daytime ride to save money.

By skipping the overpriced gondola rides during peak season, you'll save yourself from a less-than-magical experience. You can still take in Venice's famous canals without the hordes, clamor, and exorbitant costs if you prepare ahead of time.

2. AVOID EATING AT RESTAURANTS IN PIAZZA SAN MARCO

Piazza San Marco (St. Mark's Square) is one of Venice's most famous landmarks, known for its stunning architecture and vibrant atmosphere. However, the restaurants and cafés that line this iconic square are notorious for being overpriced and often cater exclusively to tourists. Even though the location is lovely, eating here may leave you with a bad meal and a hollow wallet.

WHY SHOULD YOU AVOID IT?

The restaurants in and around Piazza San Marco often charge exorbitant prices for mediocre food. A simple coffee or sandwich can cost double or triple what you'd pay elsewhere in Venice, and full meals are even more expensive. To further increase the bill, some restaurants also tack on expensive cover charges or fees for dining outside. When sitting in the square, tourists frequently report having to pay €20 or more just for a coffee.

Additionally, the food quality at these establishments tends to be geared toward mass tourism, with menus that lack authenticity and flavor. Instead of the real Venetian food for which the city is renowned, you're more likely to find boring, expensive pasta or pizza.

WHAT TO DO INSTEAD?

- **Explore Side Streets for Better Dining:** A short distance from Piazza San Marco, there are cozy, family-owned trattorias that serve far superior cuisine at affordable costs. These hidden gems serve authentic Venetian cuisines, such as **risotto al nero di sepia** (squid ink risotto) or **sarde in saor** (sweet and sour sardines), without the inflated prices you'll find in the square.
- **Visit Bacari for a True Venetian Experience:** For a more authentic experience, head to a local **bacaro**, a traditional Venetian wine bar. Bacari serves **cicchetti**, small plates of local specialties like **baccalà mantecato** (creamed cod), or marinated seafood paired with a glass of local wine. It's a wonderful way to eat, mingle with locals, and stay away from tourist hotspots.
- **Grab Coffee Away from the Square:** If you want to enjoy a coffee without breaking the bank, venture away from the main tourist areas. Coffee in Italy is generally inexpensive, so if you're paying more than a few euros, you're likely in a tourist trap. Head to a café away from the square for a better deal.

ADDITIONAL TIPS

- **Check the Menu for Cover Charges:** Some restaurants in Venice, especially in tourist areas, add service fees or cover charges. Before settling in, always make sure to check the menu for these costs.
- **Don't Pay Extra for Music:** Some restaurants in Piazza San Marco charge an additional fee if live music is playing. Consider this additional expense before selecting a table.

By avoiding the overpriced restaurants in Piazza San Marco, you'll save money and enjoy a more authentic Venetian dining experience. You can experience Venice authentically without having to pay exorbitant tourist fees by exploring the city's back lanes and neighborhood restaurants.

3. DON'T FEED THE PIGEONS

Piazza San Marco, often filled with flocks of pigeons, has long attracted tourists looking to take photos of themselves feeding these birds. It is, however, not only discouraged but also illegal to feed the pigeons. Venice has implemented strict laws to control the pigeon population, and violating them could lead to fines.

WHY SHOULD YOU AVOID IT?

Feeding pigeons in Venice is against the law, and those caught in the act face fines ranging from €50 to €500. Since feeding pigeons damages the city's historic buildings and monuments, the local government has outlawed feeding them for many years. Pigeon droppingSince feeding pigeons damages the city's historic buildings and monuments, the local government has outlawed feeding them for many years.s are highly acidic and have caused significant wear on Venice's marble and stone facades, leading to expensive repairs.

Beyond the potential fines, feeding pigeons encourages them to flock around tourists, which can be unpleasant and unsanitary. These birds can become aggressive when seeking food, swarming anyone who offers them a snack. This interferes with other visitors' attempts to appreciate the beauty of Piazza San Marco and the surrounding landmarks in addition to your own.

WHAT TO DO INSTEAD?

- **Admire the Pigeons from a Distance:** Venice's pigeons are part of the city's atmosphere, and you can enjoy watching them as they fly around Piazza San Marco without interacting directly with them. You can still capture the essence of Venice without breaking any laws if you take pictures from a distance without giving them any food.
- **Explore Other Parts of Venice:** Try visiting less crowded parts of the city if the St. Mark's Square pigeon crowds are too much for you. Venice is full of hidden corners, picturesque canals, and quiet squares where you can enjoy the beauty of the city without the flocks of birds.
- **Respect Local Rules:** Always be mindful of the local regulations, especially

in a city like Venice, where maintaining the integrity of the historic environment is crucial. Following the rules contributes to keeping the city beautiful for upcoming tourist generations.

ADDITIONAL TIPS

- **Watch for Signs**: In Piazza San Marco, there are clear signs indicating the ban on feeding pigeons. Take note of them to avoid any misunderstanding.
- **Protect Your Food**: Pigeons are often on the lookout for food, so be careful with any snacks or meals you're enjoying in public spaces to avoid attracting them.

By avoiding feeding the pigeons, you'll contribute to the preservation of Venice's architectural beauty and avoid hefty fines. It is best to enjoy the city's charm without having to deal with hostile flocks and the possible harm they may cause.

4. BEWARE OF FAKE MURANO GLASS

Venice is famous for its stunning Murano glass, hand-crafted on the nearby island of Murano. However, many of the glass items sold in the tourist areas of Venice, especially around major attractions, are cheap imitations rather than the real deal. You can save money by avoiding these fakes and buying inferior goods instead of wasting it on them.

WHY SHOULD YOU AVOID IT?

Many shops and street vendors in Venice sell mass-produced, low-quality glass items under the label of "Murano glass." These fakes are often made outside of Italy and lack the craftsmanship that true Murano glass is known for. In spite of this, they are priced as though they were real, which causes many tourists to overpay for fake glass.

Buying fake glass not only means you're spending more than the item is worth, but you're also missing out on owning a true piece of Venetian art. Murano glass is known for its quality, tradition, and the skill required to make it. Fake items don't carry that heritage.

WHAT TO DO INSTEAD?

- **Visit the Island of Murano:** To make sure you're purchasing genuine Murano glass, it's best to travel to the island. Many glassmakers offer tours of their workshops, where you can see the glassblowing process and buy directly from the source. This guarantees you're purchasing genuine Murano glass.
- **Look for Certification:** Authentic Murano glass frequently has an authenticity certificate attached to it. When shopping for glass in Venice, ask the seller for this certificate, which verifies that the item was made in Murano. Reputable shops will have these available.
- **Avoid Street Vendors:** Street vendors in Venice often sell cheap imitations. If you want a real piece of Murano glass, skip the vendors and head to established stores or galleries. These locations are more likely to sell authentic goods.

ADDITIONAL TIPS

- **Check the Price:** Authentic Murano glass is not cheap. If the price seems too good to be true, it probably is. Because authentic Murano glass requires more skill to make, the cost is higher.
- **Examine the Craftsmanship:** Genuine Murano glass has a refined, high-quality finish. Look closely at the details—if the item looks poorly made or has imperfections, it's likely not authentic.

By avoiding fake Murano glass and shopping wisely, you can take home a true piece of Venetian art, supporting local artisans and preserving the city's rich craft traditions.

5. AVOID STAYING IN THE CITY CENTER

Venice's city center, particularly areas around Piazza San Marco and the Rialto Bridge, is the heart of tourist activity. While staying close to these famous landmarks might seem appealing, it often comes with a high price and some significant drawbacks. It might not be the best idea to spend your stay in the city center due to high lodging prices and throngs of people.

WHY SHOULD YOU AVOID IT?

Accommodations in Venice's city center are notoriously expensive, especially during peak tourist seasons. Hotels and rental properties near major attractions tend to charge premium prices, often for smaller, less comfortable rooms. In addition to being expensive, lodging in the city center means putting up with continual crowds, which can make it challenging to take advantage of Venice's more sedate, peaceful aspects.

The heavy tourist traffic in these areas also drives up the prices of nearby restaurants, shops, and services, so even daily activities like dining out or buying souvenirs can cost significantly more than they would in less crowded areas of the city.

WHAT TO DO INSTEAD?

- **Stay in Mestre or Lido:** Consider making hotel reservations in Mestre, a mainland town that is accessible from Venice with a quick bus or train ride. Accommodations here are much more affordable, and public transportation can get you into Venice quickly. Alternatively, you could stay on the Lido, a peaceful island that offers easy access to Venice by Vaporetto while providing a quieter, more relaxed environment.
- **Explore Cannaregio or Dorsoduro:** If you prefer to stay within Venice itself but want to avoid the chaos of the city center, look for accommodations in quieter neighborhoods like Cannaregio or Dorsoduro. These less-touristy neighborhoods provide more genuine Venetian experiences, more affordable lodging, and convenient access to the city's top attractions.
- **Book Accommodations Early:** Venice is a popular destination year-round, so booking your accommodation early can help you find a place outside the city center at a better price. You'll have more choices when it

comes to visiting the more sedate parts of the city if you plan ahead.

ADDITIONAL TIPS

- **Check Transportation Options**: If you plan to stay outside of the city center, be sure there are public transportation options nearby. Venice's water buses (Vaporetto) and trains are reliable and make it easy to access the main attractions.
- **Avoid Peak Season Stays**: If possible, visit Venice in the off-season (November to February) when crowds are thinner and accommodations are more affordable.

By avoiding overpriced accommodations in the city center, you can save money, experience a more peaceful side of Venice, and still be within easy reach of its famous landmarks.

6. AVOID THE RIALTO BRIDGE AT PEAK TIMES

One of Venice's most recognizable landmarks is the Rialto Bridge, which connects two historic areas of the city and provides breathtaking views of the Grand Canal. However, visiting this famous bridge during peak tourist hours can be a frustrating and crowded experience, diminishing the magic of one of Venice's most picturesque spots.

WHY SHOULD YOU AVOID IT?

During the middle of the day, especially in the high tourist season, the Rialto Bridge becomes packed with visitors trying to take photos or simply cross from one side of the Grand Canal to the other. It gets hard to appreciate the view or even to walk around freely because the little pedestrian area fills up so quickly. The crowds can also attract pickpockets, who take advantage of distracted tourists.

In addition to the congestion, the shops lining the bridge often sell overpriced souvenirs, targeting tourists passing through. The overall atmosphere can feel more like a busy shopping district than a serene Venetian experience.

WHAT TO DO INSTEAD?

- **Visit Early or Late:** If you visit the Rialto Bridge, schedule your visit for early in the morning or late at night to avoid the crowds. During these quieter hours, you'll have more space to appreciate the stunning views of the Grand Canal and take photos without the large crowds. The bridge is particularly beautiful at sunrise or in the soft glow of evening light.
- **Admire the Bridge from Afar:** From the water or along the Grand Canal's banks, you can get some of the best views of the Rialto Bridge. Consider taking a Vaporetto ride along the canal to see the bridge from a different perspective or find a quiet spot nearby to admire it from a distance without battling the crowds.
- **Explore Other Bridges:** Although the Rialto Bridge is the most well-known, Venice is home to a number of other stunning, less-traveled bridges. The **Ponte dell'Accademia** offers great views of the Grand Canal, and **Ponte dei Sospiri** (Bridge of Sighs) is another iconic Venetian landmark worth visiting.

ADDITIONAL TIPS

- **Watch Your Belongings:** The crowded nature of the Rialto Bridge makes it a hotspot for pickpockets, so keep your valuables secure and be aware of your surroundings.
- **Skip the Souvenir Shops:** The shops on the bridge often sell overpriced trinkets. Look into the markets and artisan stores in the more tranquil areas of the city for better deals and quality.

By avoiding the Rialto Bridge during peak hours, you can enjoy a more peaceful and rewarding experience, taking in Venice's beauty without the hassle of large crowds and overpriced shops.

7. DON'T BUY CHEAP SOUVENIRS FROM STREET VENDORS

Venice is famous for its beautiful craftsmanship, including intricate masks, glass from Murano, and fine lace from Burano. However, many street vendors around tourist-heavy areas sell cheap, mass-produced souvenirs that lack the authenticity and quality Venice is known for. Although it could be alluring to grab a quick memento, these things are frequently poorly made and overpriced.

WHY SHOULD YOU AVOID IT?

The masks, glass trinkets, and other souvenirs sold by street vendors in Venice are often cheaply made, mass-produced, and not representative of true Venetian craftsmanship. These products are usually imported and don't have the same meticulous attention to detail as handcrafted goods made by regional artisans. While the prices may seem lower than in shops, you're likely paying more for an inferior product that won't last.

Additionally, purchasing these items supports a system that undermines local artisans who rely on their craft for their livelihood. By buying mass-produced souvenirs, tourists contribute to the decline of traditional craftsmanship that Venice is famous for.

WHAT TO DO INSTEAD?

- **Shop at Artisan Stores:** Small, neighborhood stores in Venice are a great place to find genuine, handcrafted goods like Murano glass, jewelry, and masks. These shops often have a higher price tag, but the quality and craftsmanship are far superior. You'll be supporting local artisans and taking home a meaningful souvenir that reflects Venice's rich cultural heritage.
- **Visit the Islands of Murano and Burano:** For authentic glass and lace, take a trip to Murano or Burano, where these crafts originated. Visiting these islands allows you to see the artisans at work and buy directly from

the source. Even though the cost is higher, you'll be purchasing a genuine work of Venetian art.

- **Look for Certified Shops:** Many shops that sell authentic Murano glass or Venetian masks will provide certification proving that the items are handmade in Venice. Look for this certification to ensure you're buying a genuine product.

ADDITIONAL TIPS

- **Avoid Bargain Prices**: If a souvenir seems too cheap to be authentic, it probably is. Genuine Venetian masks or Murano glass are expensive due to the craftsmanship involved.
- **Support Local Markets**: Explore local markets and art fairs where Venetian artisans sell their handmade goods. These locations frequently have more genuine and distinctive souvenirs than the booths next to tourist attractions.

By avoiding cheap, mass-produced souvenirs from street vendors, you'll bring home a piece of Venice that truly represents its cultural and artistic traditions while supporting the local economy.

8. AVOID USING WATER TAXIS IF YOU'RE ON A BUDGET

Venice's waterways are its lifeblood, and getting around by boat is part of the city's charm. While water taxis may seem like a convenient option for zipping around the canals, they come with a steep price. Water taxis can easily turn from being an affordable luxury to an expensive indulgence for tourists on a tight budget.

WHY SHOULD YOU AVOID IT?

Water taxis in Venice are one of the most expensive ways to get around. A short trip can easily cost over €100, especially if you're traveling with luggage or at night. Some travelers have reported paying even more for longer trips or during busy times. The fares are often unregulated, and additional fees can add up quickly. If you're on a budget, this mode of transport can eat into your spending money fast.

Furthermore, the majority of trips in Venice can be completed without a water taxi because many areas are best explored on foot or by public transportation. The city is relatively small, and most attractions are within walking distance of one another.

WHAT TO DO INSTEAD?

- **Use the Vaporetto (Water Bus):** The Vaporetto is Venice's public water bus service and a much cheaper alternative to water taxis. For €7.50, you can take a single ride along the Grand Canal or out to nearby islands like Murano or Burano. For extended visits, think about getting a travel pass, which is a terrific deal for seeing the city and grants unlimited rides for a predetermined number of days.
- **Walk as Much as Possible:** Many of Venice's most breathtaking sights are easily accessible on foot, as the city is designed with pedestrians in mind. Walking through Venice's narrow streets and over its charming bridges is one of the best ways to experience the city's unique character and discover hidden gems.
- **Take a Traghetto for Short Canal Crossings:** If you want to have a gondola experience without paying a high price, take a traghetto. These shared gondolas cross the Grand Canal at various points and only cost around €2. It's a quick, affordable way to enjoy a gondola ride and cross the canal without paying for a full private tour.

ADDITIONAL TIPS

- **Plan Your Route:** Venice's public transportation system is well-connected, so plan your trips using the Vaporetto to get around efficiently. Most major attractions are easily accessible by water bus.
- **Be Aware of Taxi Scams:** If you do choose to take a water taxi, make sure to agree on a price beforehand and avoid any unlicensed operators to prevent being overcharged.

By opting for the Vaporetto or exploring Venice on foot, you'll save money while still enjoying the city's iconic waterways and stunning views. While they can be a luxury, water taxis are not essential to having the best possible Venetian experience.

9. STEER CLEAR OF OVERPRICED GELATO STANDS

Venice is known for its delicious gelato, just like many other parts of Italy. However, not all gelato stands are created equal, and the ones located near major tourist attractions tend to sell overpriced, low-quality gelato that's more about drawing in tourists than offering an authentic Italian treat. Being aware of the top gelato locations can save you from being let down and from going over budget.

WHY SHOULD YOU AVOID IT?

Many gelato stands near popular spots like St. Mark's Square, the Rialto Bridge, or the Grand Canal charge inflated prices for a scoop of gelato. In some cases, tourists have reported paying up to €10 for a cone that's not even of good quality. These tourist-trap gelato stands often use artificial ingredients, resulting in overly sweet, synthetic-tasting gelato that lacks the fresh, creamy flavor of the real thing.

In an effort to draw customers, some vendors also heap their gelato high in vibrant colors; however, this typically indicates that the gelato is mass-produced and contains artificial additives rather than being made fresh on the spot.

WHAT TO DO INSTEAD?

- **Look for Natural Colors:** Authentic gelato is made with natural ingredients, so the colors should reflect that. Avoid gelato that's unnaturally bright or neon-colored. Banana gelato, for instance, ought to be a soft yellow rather than a fake bright yellow. It's more likely to be made with real, fresh ingredients if the color is more natural.
- **Find Gelato Stored in Covered Metal Tins:** Premium gelato is frequently kept in lidded metal tins to maintain its texture and freshness. If you see

gelato piled high in plastic tubs, it's likely mass-produced and filled with additives to enhance its appearance. Seek out gelaterias where the gelato is covered and stored properly.
- **Explore Side Streets for Better Gelato:** The greatest gelato, like many other things in Venice, is frequently discovered outside of the busy tourist districts. Venture a few streets away from the main attractions to find smaller, family-owned gelaterias where locals go. These shops are more likely to serve fresh, handmade gelato at reasonable prices.

ADDITIONAL TIPS

- **Check the Price Before Ordering:** Always check the price before you order. If a gelato stand doesn't have prices displayed, it's a good sign you may be overcharged.
- **Ask for Seasonal Flavors:** Authentic gelaterias often use seasonal ingredients, so ask for flavors that reflect what's in season. This guarantees that fresh, premium produce is used to make the gelato.

By avoiding the overpriced gelato stands near tourist hubs and seeking out authentic gelaterias, you'll enjoy a true taste of Italy's favorite frozen treat without overpaying or compromising on quality.

10. AVOID LUGGING LARGE SUITCASES THROUGH VENICE'S NARROW STREETS

Venice is an exquisite city that presents a distinct challenge when it comes to traveling with bags. The city's narrow, winding streets, numerous bridges, and absence of cars make dragging large suitcases a frustrating and difficult task. Planning ahead can save you both time and hassle.

WHY SHOULD YOU AVOID IT?

Venice's streets are often very narrow, crowded, and filled with steps and bridges that can make it difficult to move with large, heavy suitcases. It can be tiresome to carry your bags up and down stairs on several of the bridges, especially in the warm weather of Venice or when there is a lot of tourist traffic. Rolling a large suitcase on the city's cobblestone streets is not only impractical but also noisy and disruptive to other pedestrians.

Additionally, Venice is full of winding alleyways, and getting lost is easy, especially with heavy luggage in tow. If your accommodation is far from the main entry points like Piazzale Roma or Santa Lucia Station, you might have a long, difficult walk ahead of you.

WHAT TO DO INSTEAD?

- **Pack Light:** Traveling light is the best way to avoid having trouble with your luggage in Venice. Choose a backpack or a smaller suitcase so you can cross the bridges with ease. A compact, easy-to-carry bag will save you the headache of lugging a large suitcase through the city's winding streets.
- **Use Luggage Services:** For a fee, Venice provides luggage transport services to transfer your bags from the major transportation hubs to your lodging. These services are particularly helpful if you're staying far from major entry points or if you have heavy bags. This option allows you to navigate Venice's streets and bridges without the burden of carrying luggage.
- **Book Accommodations Near Transport Hubs:** If you're traveling with larger luggage, consider booking accommodations closer to transport hubs like Piazzale Roma or the Santa Lucia Train Station. This makes leaving and arriving in Venice much simpler and reduces the amount of walking you'll need to do with your bags.

ADDITIONAL TIPS

- **Use a Backpack or Carry-On:** A backpack or small carry-on suitcase is easier to manage on Venice's streets than a large, rolling suitcase.
- **Travel During Off-Peak Hours:** If possible, try to arrive in Venice early in the morning or late in the evening when the streets are less crowded. This will make navigating with luggage much less stressful.

By packing light or using luggage services, you can avoid the hassle of dragging heavy suitcases through Venice's narrow streets and enjoy your time in this magical city with less stress.

Venice is a timeless beauty that enthralls tourists with its rich culture, old buildings, and canals. But it's simple to fall victim to tourist traps that take away from its allure. By being mindful of when and where to visit, avoiding overpriced services, and seeking out authentic local experiences, you can uncover a Venice that many travelers miss.

Skip the crowded gondola rides, overpriced gelato, and cheap souvenirs, and instead explore the quieter streets, visit the islands where artisans still craft glass and lace by hand, and enjoy Venetian cuisine away from the bustling tourist hubs. Those who take the time to look past Venice's obvious attractions and discover its hidden gems will be rewarded.

With this guide, you're equipped to navigate Venice like a savvy traveler, ensuring your time in this enchanting city is filled with genuine experiences and lasting memories.

FLORENCE

Florence, the birthplace of the Renaissance, is a city rich in history, art, and culture. Known for its world-renowned museums, stunning architecture, and cobblestone streets, Florence is home to some of Italy's most iconic landmarks, including the Duomo, the Uffizi Gallery, and Michelangelo's David. With its breathtaking art, charming piazzas, and incredible food, Florence consistently ranks as one of the most beloved destinations for travelers worldwide.

However, like any popular city, Florence can also be filled with tourist traps, long lines, and overpriced services that may detract from the city's true beauty and authenticity. Travelers often find themselves in crowded areas or paying more for goods and experiences that don't reflect the true essence of Florentine life. It's simple to get drawn into Florence's more tourist-oriented side, from street sellers offering inexpensive leather goods to eateries with "tourist menus" serving mediocre fare.

But there's another side to the city, one that's filled with local charm and hidden gems, waiting to be discovered by those who take the time to explore beyond the tourist hotspots. Florence is a city best experienced at a slower pace—wandering through its narrow streets, getting lost in its art, and savoring its delicious cuisine.

This guide will teach you how to experience Florence like a local and help you steer clear of common pitfalls.

Whether it's skipping the overpriced markets, finding the best gelato away from the crowds, or discovering quiet corners with breathtaking views, you'll learn how to appreciate the authentic side of Florence. The city's true magic lies in its balance between the grandeur of its historical landmarks and the quiet beauty of its everyday life.

With the advice in this guide, you can enjoy Florence's timeless charm without falling into the common tourist traps, making your trip both unforgettable and authentically Florentine. Florence is a city to be savored, not rushed.

1. SKIP MARKET VENDORS SELLING CHEAP LEATHER

Florence has a centuries-old reputation for creating high-quality leather goods, and the city is well known for its leather craftsmanship. Many visitors come to Florence expecting to find beautifully crafted bags, jackets, belts, and wallets to take home as souvenirs. However, while you'll find plenty of leather goods for sale, not all of them are as authentic as they seem—especially at the popular street markets.

WHY SHOULD YOU AVOID IT?

The San Lorenzo Market and other street stalls around Florence are filled with vendors selling leather goods, often at what seem like bargain prices. However, many of the items sold here are mass-produced, imported from outside Italy, and lack the quality that Florence's renowned leather workshops are known for. Often, the workmanship is subpar, with jackets and bags constructed of cheap materials or even synthetic leather passed off as real.

Additionally, while the prices may seem like a steal, the reality is that many of these items won't last long due to subpar materials and manufacturing. What you thought was a good deal could turn into a disappointment once the item starts to wear down after a short time.

WHAT TO DO INSTEAD?

- **Visit Reputable Leather Shops:** For genuine Florentine leather, avoid market stalls and instead visit established leather shops or workshops. Many of these stores offer high-quality, handmade leather goods that are crafted by local artisans using traditional methods. Shops such as **Scuola del Cuoio** or **Franco's Leather Factory** are well-known for their authentic, well-crafted products. While you'll pay more than you would at a market, you'll be investing in a piece that will last for years and carry the

true essence of Florentine craftsmanship.
- **Look for Certification:** Authentic leather shops in Florence often provide certificates of authenticity for their products, verifying that the leather is locally sourced and handcrafted. When shopping, find out about this certification to make sure the products you're buying are real leather.
- **Shop in Less Touristy Areas:** Look into smaller stores in less-traveled areas to avoid expensive or subpar products. Areas like **Oltrarno**, across the river from the main tourist sites, are known for their artisan workshops, where you can find unique leather goods made by skilled craftsmen.

ADDITIONAL TIPS

- **Inspect the Quality:** Real leather has a distinct smell and texture. Be sure to examine the stitching, check for any flaws, and feel the leather to ensure it's genuine. You can be pretty sure that a price is too good to be true.
- **Avoid Pressure to Buy:** Market vendors are often skilled at pressuring tourists into making quick purchases. Don't feel pressured to purchase something that doesn't live up to your expectations; instead, take your time.

By avoiding the temptation to buy cheap leather from market vendors and instead seeking out authentic shops, you'll take home a true piece of Florence's artisanal heritage. When it comes to the famous leather goods made in this city, quality is definitely worth the extra money.

2. AVOID EATING NEAR PIAZZA DEL DUOMO

Piazza del Duomo is the heart of Florence and home to some of the city's most iconic landmarks, including the majestic Cathedral of Santa Maria del Fiore (the Duomo), the Baptistery of St. John, and Giotto's Bell Tower. Travelers should not miss this must-see area, but if you're looking for somewhere to eat, steer clear of the cafés and restaurants that are right around the square.

WHY SHOULD YOU AVOID IT?

The restaurants around the Duomo frequently serve only tourists, which drives up costs and degrades the quality of the food. These establishments rely on the constant flow of visitors rather than returning locals, so they need more incentive to serve authentic, high-quality dishes. Meals in these restaurants are often overpriced, and portions may be smaller than what you'd find in less touristy areas.

Apart from the exorbitant costs, you might encounter menus that prioritize satisfying the tastes of tourists over providing authentic Tuscan fare. Many of these places serve watered-down versions of Italian classics or generic dishes that lack the rich flavors Florence is known for. Paying €20 or more for an average pasta or pizza when you could enjoy a much better meal just a few streets away is a common mistake.

WHAT TO DO INSTEAD?

- **Venture Away from the Tourist Hub:** A short stroll from Piazza del Duomo will take you to a number of fantastic eateries that serve real Tuscan cuisine at much more affordable costs. Areas like **Santa Croce** or **San Frediano** are less crowded with tourists and home to small, family-run trattorias that serve flavorful, traditional dishes.
- **Look for Trattorias Where Locals Dine:** Locals at the tables are the best sign of a good restaurant in Florence. Trattorias and osterias, where Florentines gather for lunch or dinner, are more likely to serve genuine Tuscan fare at fair prices. Authentic dishes like **ribollita** (a Tuscan bread soup) or **bistecca alla Fiorentina** (Florentine steak) can be found at these local gems.
- **Ask for Recommendations:** Ask locals or store owners for restaurant recommendations if you're not sure where to eat. Florentines take pride in their food and are often happy to point you toward a trattoria serving real, local dishes.

ADDITIONAL TIPS

- **Avoid Menus in Multiple Languages**: If a restaurant has a menu available in several languages, especially English, it's usually a sign that it caters to tourists. For a more genuine experience, seek out establishments that have an Italian-only menu and keep things simple.
- **Watch Out for Cover Charges**: Some tourist-heavy restaurants near the Duomo add high cover charges for simply sitting at a table, especially if it's outside. Always make an inquiry or check the menu before settling in.

By skipping the touristy restaurants near Piazza del Duomo and exploring Florence's quieter streets, you'll not only save money but also experience the city's incredible food as the locals do. Finding genuine, excellent Tuscan food may be greatly improved by taking a quick stroll.

3. STEER CLEAR OF LONG LINES AT THE UFFIZI GALLERY

One of Florence's most well-known and significant art galleries, the Uffizi Gallery is home to well-known pieces by Renaissance masters like Michelangelo, Leonardo da Vinci, and Botticelli. It's a must-see for anyone visiting Florence, but its popularity often means long lines and crowded galleries, which can turn a highly anticipated visit into a frustrating experience.

WHY SHOULD YOU AVOID IT?

During peak tourist seasons, especially in the summer, the lines to enter the Uffizi Gallery can stretch for hours. Waiting in the hot sun, especially in Florence's sweltering summer months, can quickly become exhausting, leaving you tired before you even step inside the museum. Furthermore, once you're inside, the galleries can get crowded, which makes it challenging to appreciate the artwork to the fullest without getting overwhelmed by the number of people.

Long lines are a common problem at the Uffizi because it has a limited capacity for visitors, and many tourists arrive without pre-booking tickets, hoping to get in on the day of their visit. If the tickets sell out, this results in lengthy lines and frequently disappointment.

WHAT TO DO INSTEAD?

- **Book Tickets Online in Advance:** The easiest way to avoid long lines at the Uffizi is to purchase your tickets online in advance. With the timed entry system the Uffizi offers, you can book a particular window of time for your visit. By booking ahead, you can skip the general admission line and head straight into the museum at your reserved time. This ensures that you'll be able to see the art without the frustration of a long wait.
- **Opt for a Guided Tour with Skip-the-Line Access:** Taking a guided tour that offers skip-the-line access is an additional choice. Many tours offer small-group experiences with an art historian or local guide who can provide deeper insights into the masterpieces you'll see. These tours not only allow you to bypass the long lines but also enrich your understanding of the art and its significance.
- **Visit During Off-Peak Times:** If you can't make a reservation in advance, think about going to the Uffizi early in the morning or late in the afternoon when it's less crowded. Weekdays are generally less crowded than weekends, and the museum is often quieter during the off-season, from November to February.

ADDITIONAL TIPS

- **Combine Your Uffizi Ticket with Other Museums:** Uffizi offers combined tickets that include entry to other important sites like the **Palazzo Pitti** and the **Boboli Gardens**. These tickets are incredibly affordable and spare you from having to wait in long lines while traveling.
- **Take Breaks in the Museum:** The Uffizi is large and can be overwhelming. Take advantage of the seating areas and café within the museum to rest and recharge during your visit.

By planning ahead and avoiding the long lines, you'll be able to enjoy the incredible art at the Uffizi Gallery without the stress of waiting. If you have a little foresight, you can make the most out of your visit and truly appreciate the masterpieces inside.

4. DON'T BUY SOUVENIRS FROM SHOPS IN TOURIST AREAS

Florence is famous for its art, craftsmanship, and unique souvenirs, but the shops located near major tourist attractions, like Piazza del Duomo and the Ponte Vecchio, often sell mass-produced, low-quality items at inflated prices. These stores sell generic mementos that don't accurately capture Florence's genuine artistic and cultural heritage in order to satisfy the city's steady stream of tourists.

WHY SHOULD YOU AVOID IT?

The most well-known tourist destinations in Florence have souvenir shops that frequently stock mass-produced art prints, imitation sculptures, magnets, and inexpensive leather goods. These items are frequently imported and lack the quality and authenticity that make Florence's crafts so special. While it might be tempting to pick up a quick memento, you'll likely end up paying much more than the item is worth.

In addition, many of these items are made to look like authentic Florentine products—especially leather goods or art—but are actually mass-produced in factories. This lessens the souvenir's value and lessens support for regional artists who make a living from their craft.

WHAT TO DO INSTEAD?

- **Seek Out Local Artisans:** There is a long history of exquisite handicrafts in Florence, where a large number of local craftspeople produce jewelry, ceramics, leather bags, and artwork. Look for small shops and workshops, particularly in less touristy areas like **Oltrarno** or near **Santa Croce**, where you can find unique, high-quality items made by local artists. These souvenirs carry the true spirit of Florence and will be much more meaningful than mass-produced trinkets.

- **Visit Artisanal Markets:** There are numerous local markets in Florence where craftspeople sell their handmade goods. Markets like the **Mercato di Sant'Ambrogio** or the monthly **Mercato delle Pulci** (flea market) offer a variety of unique, locally made items. Shopping at these markets not only supports local craftsmen but also gives you the chance to take home something truly authentic.
- **Buy Original Art:** Florence is an artist's city, and buying a piece of original art from a local gallery or directly from an artist is a wonderful way to remember your trip. Original artwork, whether it be a miniature painting, a sculpture, or a pen-and-paper sketch, creates a sentimental and intimate memento.

ADDITIONAL TIPS

- **Avoid Replica David Statues**: Replica statues of Michelangelo's David are common in tourist shops, but they're often poorly made. Go to a respectable gallery or artisan store if you're looking for a fine replica or artwork inspired by the David.
- **Bargain Smartly at Markets**: While some haggling is expected at markets, be respectful and aware that handmade items often reflect hours of skilled labor. Strike a reasonable price without undervaluing the artisans' labor.

By skipping the touristy souvenir shops and seeking out local artisans, you'll not only take home a higher-quality souvenir but also support the traditional craftsmanship that makes Florence so unique. Your purchases will capture the authentic spirit of Florence, adding to the specialness and durability of your mementos.

5. AVOID BUYING DAVID REPLICAS FROM STREET VENDORS

Since David by Michelangelo is one of the most famous sculptures in the entire world, it makes sense that a lot of visitors would want to bring home a memento that was inspired by this masterwork. However, the cheap David replicas sold by street vendors and souvenir shops near the Accademia and other tourist-heavy areas are often poorly made and overpriced. These items fail to capture the artistry and significance of the original statue.

WHY SHOULD YOU AVOID IT?

Many of the David replicas sold by street vendors are mass-produced from low-quality materials such as plastic or plaster. These replicas are often poorly detailed and made quickly to meet the high demand of tourists rather than being crafted with care and precision. They are usually sold for exorbitant prices despite their poor quality just because they look like the well-known statue by Michelangelo.

In addition, buying these knockoff replicas does little to support Florence's renowned artistic traditions or the local economy. You'll be leaving with a cheap memento that doesn't accurately capture the genuine artistry and skill for which Florence is renowned, and it probably won't be very charming or durable.

WHAT TO DO INSTEAD?

- **Purchase from Reputable Artisan Shops:** If you're looking for a high-quality David replica or a piece of art inspired by Michelangelo's work, visit a reputable gallery or artisan shop. Many local shops specialize in reproductions of Florence's famous artworks, using better materials and superior craftsmanship. These stores frequently sell marble or bronze replicas of David, which are far more detailed and long-lasting than the plastic ones that street vendors sell.
- **Buy Original Art or Sculptures:** Investing in an original artwork or sculpture created by a local artist can make for a more distinctive and personalized memento. Florence is filled with galleries showcasing contemporary art and sculptures, often inspired by the Renaissance. Buying original art supports local artists and provides a meaningful and one-of-a-kind keepsake from your trip.
- **Visit Workshops Where Replicas Are Made:** In Florence, some

workshops specialize in creating high-quality replicas of famous sculptures, including the David. You can observe the manufacturing process in action by visiting these workshops, which also ensures that you are purchasing a genuine, expertly crafted replica straight from the creators.

ADDITIONAL TIPS

- **Check the Materials**: Verify the material if you do choose to purchase a replica. Marble or stone replicas will be more expensive, but they're also more durable and a better reflection of the original statue.
- **Avoid Impulse Buys**: Avoid impulsively purchasing a copy from the first seller you come across.. Take your time to explore your options and ensure you're getting something of quality.

By avoiding low-quality David replicas sold by street vendors and seeking out authentic reproductions or original art, you'll take home a meaningful souvenir that reflects Florence's rich artistic heritage. Purchasing a more durable piece that accurately captures the splendor of Michelangelo's masterwork is well worth the investment.

6. AVOID RESTAURANTS OFFERING "TOURIST MENUS"

Florence is known for its incredible cuisine, from hearty Tuscan soups to the famous bistecca alla Fiorentina. However, many restaurants located in tourist-heavy areas offer "tourist menus," which cater to visitors rather than locals. These menus frequently offer overpriced, subpar cuisine, giving guests a less-than-genuine eating experience.

WHY SHOULD YOU AVOID IT?

"Tourist menu" restaurants usually offer simplified Italian meals that aren't as authentic or flavorful as traditional Florentine fare. These menus are designed to appeal to a broad, international audience, often offering pizza, pasta, and other generic options that aren't representative of the local culinary traditions. The ingredients used are often of lower quality, and the dishes may be prepared quickly and carelessly to serve the constant flow of tourists.

Apart from the inadequate quality of food, the costs listed on tourist menus are typically more than those of a neighborhood trattoria. Restaurants targeting tourists know that visitors are often willing to pay more for convenience, but the result is often an overpriced meal that doesn't showcase the true flavors of Florence.

WHAT TO DO INSTEAD?

- **Seek Out Family-Run Trattorias:** Visit family-run trattorias for a more genuine dining experience, where you can get traditional, carefully prepared Florentine cuisine. These trattorias are often located away from the main tourist areas and offer genuine Tuscan cuisine at fair prices. Look for dishes like **ribollita** (Tuscan bread soup), **pappardelle al cinghiale** (wild boar pasta), or **bistecca alla Fiorentina** (Florentine steak) for a true taste of Florence.
- **Check the Menu Before Sitting Down:** It's a good idea to look at the menu before selecting a restaurant. If the menu is written in multiple languages and features standard tourist dishes like pizza or spaghetti bolognese, it's a sign that the restaurant is catering to tourists. Instead, look for menus that highlight local specialties and are primarily written in Italian.
- **Ask Locals for Recommendations:** Seeking advice from locals is one of the best ways to locate a delicious meal. Florentines take pride in their food and will often point you toward trattorias and osterias that offer authentic, delicious meals without the tourist trap prices.

ADDITIONAL TIPS

- **Avoid Restaurants with Aggressive Waiters:** If there's someone trying to entice you inside the restaurant from the outside, it's often a sign that the restaurant is focused on attracting tourists rather than serving quality food.
- **Look for Daily Specials:** Many local restaurants offer daily specials based on fresh, seasonal ingredients. These dishes are often the best

representation of traditional Tuscan cooking.

By skipping the tourist menus and seeking out local eateries, you'll experience the rich flavors of Florence's culinary heritage. Finding the ideal location will take some work, but the payoff is an incredible dinner that captures the essence of Tuscan cooking.

7. SKIP VISITING PIAZZALE MICHELANGELO AT MIDDAY

Piazzale Michelangelo is one of the best spots in Florence to take in a panoramic view of the city. From here, you can see the famous red-tiled rooftops, the Duomo, and the Arno River winding through the city. It's a must-visit for anyone wanting to capture the perfect photo of Florence. But going there in the middle of the day can be crowded, stuffy, and less fun.

WHY SHOULD YOU AVOID IT?

Piazzale Michelangelo is a well-liked tourist destination that can get very crowded at midday. The combination of large tour groups and individual visitors all vying for the best photo spot can make the experience feel rushed and chaotic. In the summer months, the midday heat can also be intense, leaving you uncomfortable and exhausted while you try to enjoy the view.

Furthermore, the intense midday sun can distort the colors of the cityscape, making it more difficult to get the ideal shot. You're also more likely to encounter street vendors selling overpriced souvenirs and food, further detracting from the peaceful experience that this viewpoint should offer.

WHAT TO DO INSTEAD?

- **Visit Early in the Morning or at Sunset:** Plan your visit to Piazzale Michelangelo for early in the morning or late in the evening, around sunset, for a more tranquil experience. In the morning, the crowds are smaller, and the soft light creates a beautiful atmosphere for taking photos. Sunset is another ideal time to visit, as the golden light bathes the city in a warm glow, making for stunning photos and a more relaxed vibe.

- **Consider Visiting at Night:** The view from Piazzale Michelangelo at night is equally breathtaking. With the city's lights twinkling and the Duomo illuminated, it offers a magical perspective of Florence. Visits at night are usually much quieter, so you can take in the scenery quietly.
- **Take the Walk to San Miniato al Monte:** For an even better view and fewer crowds, consider walking a bit farther up to **San Miniato al Monte**, a historic basilica located just above Piazzale Michelangelo. This location offers an equally breathtaking view, and the basilica is a lovely location well worth seeing.

ADDITIONAL TIPS

- **Bring Water and a Hat:** If you do visit during the day, be sure to bring water and protection from the sun, as there is little shade at Piazzale Michelangelo.
- **Plan Your Photos Around the Light:** The best photos are usually taken during the golden hours—early morning or just before sunset—when the light is softer and more flattering for the cityscape.

By avoiding the midday rush and opting to visit Piazzale Michelangelo during quieter, more scenic times, you'll have a far more enjoyable experience. Enjoying the stunning views of Florence in a tranquil and laid-back atmosphere is highly recommended.

8. AVOID BUYING BOTTLED WATER AT TOURIST SPOTS

Florence's warm climate and bustling streets mean staying hydrated is essential while exploring the city. However, buying bottled water from vendors or kiosks near major tourist attractions like the Duomo, Uffizi Gallery, and Ponte Vecchio can be unnecessarily expensive. You can easily avoid this expensive tourist trap because there are so many public drinking fountains available throughout the city.

WHY SHOULD YOU AVOID IT?

Tourist areas in Florence are filled with kiosks and street vendors selling bottled water, often at inflated prices. A small bottle of water from these vendors can cost anywhere from €2 to €5, depending on how close you are to a major attraction. These costs mount up quickly, particularly if you plan to spend an entire day exploring the sweltering city.

In addition to the cost, buying bottled water from vendors contributes to plastic waste, which is a growing problem in heavily visited cities like Florence. There is no longer a need to purchase bottled water because Florence has taken action to offer the public free, clean water.

WHAT TO DO INSTEAD?

- **Use Public Drinking Fountains:** Florence has several **fontanelles**, or public drinking fountains, where you can fill your water bottle for free. These fountains provide clean, safe drinking water and can be found throughout the city, including in popular areas like Piazza della Signoria and near the Boboli Gardens. All you need to do is keep a reusable water bottle with you and fill it up during the day.
- **Carry a Reusable Water Bottle:** Not only is it environmentally beneficial to bring a reusable water bottle, but it also prevents you from purchasing expensive bottled water. Florence's drinking fountains are easily accessible, and you can refill your bottle whenever needed, ensuring you stay hydrated without spending extra money.
- **Plan Your Stops Around the Fountains:** Make sure to schedule your exploration of Florence to pass by the public fountains. This way, you can take a break, refill your bottle, and stay hydrated without having to spend money in tourist-heavy areas.

ADDITIONAL TIPS

- **Look for Free Chilled Water:** Some of the **Fontanelli** even offer chilled water, perfect for hot summer days. Look for these fountains; they offer a cool, free way to stay refreshed while touring the city.
- **Avoid Buying at the Train Station:** Water prices at major transit points like the Santa Maria Novella train station are often very high. To avoid

paying too much, fill up your bottle at a fountain before going to the station.

By using Florence's public drinking fountains and carrying a reusable water bottle, you'll not only save money but also reduce plastic waste, making your visit to the city more environmentally friendly and budget-conscious.

9. DON'T TAKE TAXIS AROUND THE HISTORIC CENTER

Florence's historic center is one of the most walkable areas in Italy, with narrow cobblestone streets, pedestrian zones, and many of the city's major attractions within easy walking distance of each other. Despite this, some tourists opt for taxis, especially when unsure of the distance between locations. However, it's sometimes expensive and unnecessary to take taxis within the city center.

WHY SHOULD YOU AVOID IT?

- Florence's historic center is relatively small and easy to navigate on foot. Taking a taxi within this area is not only unnecessary but also impractical due to traffic restrictions. Many streets are designated as **ZTL** (Zona a Traffico Limitato), meaning only residents and authorized vehicles can enter. Because of this, it can be challenging for taxis to drop you off near the major attractions; as a result, you'll frequently need to walk the remaining distance.

Additionally, taxis in Florence are not cheap, especially for short trips around the center. The cost of a brief ride can easily add up, with flag drop rates and additional charges for luggage or nighttime rides. It's usually a waste of money to take a taxi in this walkable city.

WHAT TO DO INSTEAD?

- **Explore Florence on Foot:** Florence is best explored by walking. The major attractions, including the Duomo, Uffizi Gallery, Ponte Vecchio, and Palazzo Pitti, are all within a short distance of one another. Walking

through the city allows you to fully immerse yourself in the beauty of its streets, hidden alleys, and piazzas. Additionally, you'll find quaint cafés, artisan stores, and more sedate squares that you might not find in a taxi.
- **Use Public Transportation When Necessary:** For areas outside the historic center, such as **Fiesole** or **Piazzale Michelangelo**, Florence's public buses are a more affordable and convenient option. The majority of the city and its environs are served by the user-friendly bus system. For about €1.50, a single bus ticket, buses are a far more affordable option than taxis.
- **Consider Renting a Bike:** Renting a bike is an additional means of transportation in Florence. The city has several bike rental shops, and cycling through the less crowded parts of the city is a fun and efficient way to explore. However, be cautious when biking in pedestrian-heavy areas, as the streets can become crowded.

ADDITIONAL TIPS

- **Wear Comfortable Shoes**: Florence's cobblestone streets can be uneven, so wear comfortable shoes for walking. It's the greatest way to take in the charm of the city without paying needless taxi fares.
- **Plan Your Route**: With a little planning, you can map out your walking route to cover Florence's major sights in a day or two without the need for taxis or buses.

By walking through Florence's historic center, you'll not only save money on taxis but also gain a deeper appreciation for the city's rich history and architecture. You will learn more about Florence by strolling its streets than you ever would from the backseat of a taxi. Florence is a city that is best explored on foot.

10. AVOID BUYING ART FROM UNAUTHORIZED STREET ARTISTS

Famous for its Renaissance masterpieces and extensive artistic legacy, Florence is a creative city. As you walk through its beautiful streets, you'll often encounter street vendors selling paintings, sketches, or other forms of art. In contrast, this may seem like a charming way to take home a piece of Florence's creative spirit, but much of the artwork sold by unauthorized street vendors is mass-produced and lacks authenticity.

WHY SHOULD YOU AVOID IT?

Many of the paintings and sketches sold on the streets of Florence are not made by local artists but are often cheap, mass-produced copies of popular scenes and landmarks. These goods are produced fast in workshops, sometimes even outside of Italy, and offered to gullible travelers at exorbitant costs. While the art may look appealing at first glance, the materials and craftsmanship are often poor, meaning the pieces may not last long.

In addition, buying from unauthorized street vendors can sometimes be illegal, as many of these sellers do not have permits to sell their goods in public spaces. You risk supporting an underground economy while taking home something that doesn't truly represent Florence's artistic heritage.

WHAT TO DO INSTEAD?

- **Visit Local Art Galleries:** There is a strong art scene in Florence, with many galleries exhibiting the creations of contemporary and regional artists. Visiting a gallery allows you to purchase an original piece of art, directly supporting the artist and ensuring that you're taking home something truly unique. Galleries like **Galleria Tornabuoni** and **Aria Art Gallery** feature a range of styles and pieces, from modern works to those inspired by Florence's rich artistic history.
- **Explore Artisan Shops:** Many neighborhoods, especially **Oltrarno**, are known for their artisan workshops, where artists create one-of-a-kind

pieces of art. These stores sell a broad range of crafts, such as original paintings, sculptures, and hand-painted ceramics. Buying directly from these artisans ensures that you're getting high-quality, authentic art made by local hands.

- **Check for Authenticity:** If you decide to buy art from a vendor, ensure that it's original by asking the artist about their work and the techniques they use. Authentic street artists will often be happy to discuss their creative process and may even be working on new pieces as you browse. Seek out suppliers who have a large selection of original work and who showcase their tools.

ADDITIONAL TIPS

- **Avoid Mass-Produced Replicas**: Be wary of street art that looks too perfect or identical to others you've seen around town. Real artwork frequently has distinct textures and imperfections that are absent from mass-produced replicas.
- **Support Local Artists**: When possible, choose to buy from shops or galleries that showcase the work of Florentine artists. This helps maintain the city's creative culture in addition to guaranteeing that the art you purchase is authentic.

You can bring home a genuine piece of Florence's artistic history by avoiding unlicensed street sellers and looking for neighborhood galleries and artisan stores. Investing in authentic, original art is a meaningful way to remember your trip and support the talented artists who continue to make Florence a hub of creativity.

Florence is a city that dazzles with its art, history, and culture, but it's also a place where tourist traps and crowded attractions can detract from the experience. By knowing what to avoid, you can discover the authentic side of Florence—the side where local artisans craft beautiful leather goods, where family-run trattorias serve up the finest Tuscan dishes, and where the city's rich artistic heritage comes alive in quiet galleries and workshops.

Florence's true charm is found not just in its iconic landmarks but in the hidden corners, the narrow streets, and the quiet moments spent appreciating its beauty. With this guide, you'll be ready to tour Florence like an informed tourist, avoiding the pricey and disappointing attractions and taking advantage of all that the city has to offer.

Whether it's finding the perfect view of the city at sunrise, tasting authentic gelato away from the crowds, or taking home a handcrafted souvenir, your time in Florence will be all the more memorable by focusing on quality over convenience. It is best to take your time exploring Florence and to appreciate its genuineness.

MILAN

Milan, Italy's bustling metropolis, is known for being a global center of fashion, design, and finance. It's a city where history blends seamlessly with modernity, from the stunning Gothic architecture of the Duomo to cutting-edge art galleries and high-end boutiques. Travelers seeking art, history, and a taste of the finer things in life will find Milan's energy and elegance irresistible.

Milan is one of the most popular tourist destinations in Italy, but it also has its fair share of expensive attractions and tourist traps. Whether it's expensive restaurants around the Duomo, mass-produced souvenirs, or the temptation of high-end shopping districts, travelers can easily fall into common pitfalls that don't reflect the true Milanese experience.

With tips on what to miss and where to look for the real treasures in Milan, this guide will help you explore the city like a native. From avoiding crowded tourist spots to knowing where to get the best aperitivo without overpaying, you'll discover the real Milan, far beyond the glossy facades of high-end shops and tourist-heavy areas.

Milan's charm lies not just in its famous fashion scene but in its rich cultural history, vibrant local neighborhoods, and world-class food. You can take advantage of everything this chic city has to offer without falling victim to the typical tourist traps if you have a little insider knowledge.

1. AVOID SHOPPING ON CORSO VITTORIO EMANUELE II FOR CHEAP FASHION

Milan is renowned as one of the fashion capitals of the world, and its stylish streets are filled with both luxury and high-street brands. Corso Vittorio Emanuele II is one of Milan's busiest shopping streets, drawing tourists looking to indulge in the city's fashionable reputation. Nevertheless, this is not the ideal location to shop if you're looking for distinctive or reasonably priced clothing.

WHY SHOULD YOU AVOID IT?

Corso Vittorio Emanuele II is filled with high-street chain stores like Zara, H&M, and others that you can easily find in any major city around the world. While the area's bustling atmosphere and beautiful shopping arcades may draw you in, the reality is that many of the items sold here are neither unique nor priced competitively. The prices of the same fashion items are probably comparable to or higher than they would be at home.

Furthermore, because this is a very touristic area, the stores frequently raise their prices during the busiest travel seasons in order to profit from the influx of customers. What you might hope would be a great deal on Italian fashion could end up being a run-of-the-mill shopping experience with inflated price tags.

WHAT TO DO INSTEAD?

- **Explore Brera for Boutique Shopping:** If you're looking for something more unique, head to the **Brera district**. This artsy neighborhood is known for its independent boutiques and artisan shops, offering handmade accessories, Italian leather goods, and one-of-a-kind clothing pieces. Higher-quality, regionally produced clothing that is unique and much more representative of Milan's actual style can be found here.
- **Visit the Navigli for Vintage Finds:** For fashion lovers interested in vintage clothing, the **Navigli district** is a great place to explore. Known for

its vibrant atmosphere and canal-side markets, there are many vintage and used stores in this neighborhood where you can get one-of-a-kind clothing at lower costs.
- **Check Out Outlet Stores:** If you're in search of deals on designer fashion, Milan has several outlets worth visiting. Stores like **Serravalle Designer Outlet** and **Il Salvagente** offer significant discounts on luxury brands, allowing you to take home high-quality pieces without breaking the bank.

ADDITIONAL TIPS

- **Look for Local Designers:** Milan is home to many up-and-coming local designers. Seek out smaller, independent shops that showcase local talent for unique pieces you won't find anywhere else.
- **Avoid Peak Shopping Hours:** If you do decide to visit Corso Vittorio Emanuele II for window shopping, go early in the morning or later in the evening to avoid the massive crowds.

You'll have a much richer and more genuine shopping experience if you avoid the generic chain stores on Corso Vittorio Emanuele II and instead head for Milan's more distinctive shopping districts. Whether you're hunting for vintage treasures or high-end fashion, Milan's smaller boutiques and local shops offer far more than the tourist-heavy high-street stores.

2. SKIP DINING NEAR THE DUOMO

The Piazza del Duomo, with its stunning Gothic cathedral and bustling atmosphere, is one of Milan's top tourist spots. Naturally, many visitors gravitate toward the nearby restaurants and cafés, hoping to enjoy a meal with a view of this iconic landmark. But eating here usually means shelling out a lot of cash for mediocre food that is meant to impress visitors rather than providing a true taste of Milanese cuisine.

WHY SHOULD YOU AVOID IT?

Restaurants and cafés around the Duomo are notorious for being overpriced, often charging inflated prices for simple dishes like pasta or pizza. Many of these places are tourist traps, with generic menus that don't have the depth of flavor found in real Italian food. A pizza or pasta dish that might cost €8 to €10 a few streets away can easily be marked up to €20 or more in this area, and the quality often doesn't match the price.

These restaurants also tend to focus more on turnover than quality, prioritizing speed over crafting an authentic dining experience. The majority of the dishes are simplified to appeal to a wide, international audience rather than reflecting the local culinary traditions, so you're not likely to find the best of Milanese cuisine here.

WHAT TO DO INSTEAD?

- **Venture to Brera or Navigli for Authentic Dining:** A short walk away from the Duomo, the **Brera** and **Navigli** districts offer a more authentic and flavorful dining experience. These areas are filled with trattorias and osterias where locals dine, and the food is far more representative of true Milanese cooking. Dishes like **ossobuco** (braised veal shanks) and **risotto alla Milanese** are much better enjoyed in these districts, where the focus is on traditional preparation and high-quality ingredients.
- **Look for Family-Owned Trattorias:** Look for trattorias owned by families if you want to experience authentic Milanese cuisine. These smaller, often less flashy establishments serve authentic dishes made with care, and prices are more reasonable than the touristy restaurants near the Duomo.
- **Ask Locals for Recommendations:** Asking locals for their recommended restaurants is one of the best ways to locate a satisfying meal in Milan. Milanese locals know where to find the best food, and their recommendations are likely to lead you to hidden gems with authentic flavors.

ADDITIONAL TIPS

- **Check for "Tourist Menus":** Restaurants that offer menus in multiple languages or advertise "tourist menus" are often more focused on catering

- to tourists than serving authentic food. Stay away from these locations for a more satisfying meal.
- **Avoid Peak Times**: If you want to dine near the Duomo, go during off-peak hours to avoid the crowds and possibly get better service and food.

By avoiding the overpriced tourist restaurants near the Duomo and venturing just a few streets away, you'll enjoy a more authentic and affordable dining experience that showcases Milan's culinary heritage.

3. STEER CLEAR OF TOURIST SOUVENIR SHOPS NEAR MAJOR LANDMARKS

Milan is rich in history, art, and culture, making it a great city for souvenirs. However, the souvenir shops near major landmarks such as the Duomo, Galleria Vittorio Emanuele II, and Castello Sforzesco tend to sell overpriced, mass-produced items. Avoid these touristy stores if you want to bring home a genuine piece of Milanese craftsmanship and culture.

WHY SHOULD YOU AVOID IT?

The souvenir shops around Milan's most visited sites are filled with the usual trinkets—magnets, cheap leather goods, and keychains that often lack authenticity. These mass-produced items are typically imported and don't reflect Milanese craftsmanship or style. Furthermore, because the store is situated in a popular tourist destination, the prices are typically higher.

Purchasing from these stores frequently results in bringing home a generic item that can be found in any tourist destination, depriving oneself of Milan's genuine artistic quality. While it may be tempting to grab a quick souvenir from a shop near the Duomo, you'll likely pay more than the item is worth, and it won't have the same uniqueness as something crafted locally.

WHAT TO DO INSTEAD?

- **Seek Out Local Artisan Shops**: Milan is home to many talented artisans who create unique, handmade items such as jewelry, leather goods, and art. The **Brera** and **Navigli** districts are great places to explore smaller, independent shops where you can find beautiful, one-of-a-kind souvenirs. Products created by regional artists that highlight Milan's artistic spirit can be found here.

- **Visit the Markets:** If you're looking for more unique items, Milan's markets are worth exploring. **Mercato di Sant'Ambrogio** and the monthly **East Market** are fantastic places to discover handmade crafts, vintage goods, and artwork. These markets offer a far more genuine shopping experience than tourist souvenir stalls because they are crowded with local vendors selling everything from ceramics to original art.
- **Consider Fashion-Inspired Souvenirs:** Milan is a fashion capital, so consider buying a fashion-related souvenir, such as locally made scarves, accessories, or unique clothing pieces from emerging Milanese designers. These things are not only more useful and meaningful as mementos, but they also capture the essence of the city.

ADDITIONAL TIPS

- **Avoid "Made in China" Items:** Check labels to ensure the product is made locally. Many tourist shops sell imported goods, so look for items labeled "Made in Italy" to support local artisans.
- **Bargain Smartly:** If you do shop at markets, a bit of polite bargaining is often expected, but be respectful of the craft and work that goes into handmade items.

By avoiding the mass-produced souvenirs sold in tourist shops and seeking out local artisan goods, you'll take home a piece of Milan that truly reflects the city's vibrant culture and craftsmanship.

4. AVOID TAXI RIDES FOR SHORT DISTANCES

Milan is a big, energetic city, but its tourist attractions and historical center are surprisingly close together and accessible by foot or public transportation. Despite the convenience of taxis, using them for short distances within the city can be costly, unnecessary, and even slower than other options due to traffic.

WHY SHOULD YOU AVOID IT?

In Milan, taxi fares can be high, particularly for short trips within the city limits. The base fare starts around €6 during the day and can quickly increase due to traffic, waiting times, or additional fees for luggage and nighttime rides. Many tourists unknowingly take taxis for short trips that could easily be walked or reached via public transport, wasting both time and money.

Milan's city center, particularly areas like the Duomo, Galleria Vittorio Emanuele II, and La Scala, is very walkable and often faster to explore on foot. These places have heavy traffic, especially during rush hours, so walking or taking public transportation will get you to your destination more quickly than hailing a cab, which is frequently stuck in long lines.

WHAT TO DO INSTEAD?

- **Explore on Foot:** Walking is the best way to experience Milan's beauty, from its historical sites to its hidden gems. The city's main attractions are located close to one another. Strolling around allows you to experience the city at a leisurely pace and discover local cafés, shops, and landmarks you might miss in a taxi.
- **Use Public Transportation:** The metro, buses, and trams that makeup Milan's public transportation network are all reasonably priced and dependable. A single ticket costs around €2 and covers trips on all forms of transport for 90 minutes. The metro system, in particular, is fast and efficient, making it easy to travel further distances or reach more suburban areas without the cost of a taxi.
- **Consider Bike Rentals:** Renting a bike is a fantastic way to explore Milan and cover a bit more ground without having to deal with traffic or taxis. Milan is a bike-friendly city. Bike rental services, such as **BikeMi**, offer easy access to bicycles throughout the city, and you can explore at your own pace.

ADDITIONAL TIPS

- **Plan Your Route:** Before deciding on transport, check the distance to your

destination. Often, what looks far on a map may be a quick 10- or 15-minute walk.
- **Use Taxi Apps**: If you need a taxi, apps like **mytaxi** or **Uber** can help ensure you get a fair price and track your ride's route.

By avoiding taxis for short trips and opting to walk or use Milan's excellent public transport system, you'll save money, experience the city more authentically, and stay away from the traffic jams that can cause taxis in the city center to slow down.

5. DON'T VISIT THE NAVIGLI DISTRICT ON WEEKEND EVENINGS

The Navigli District, known for its picturesque canals and lively atmosphere, is a must-visit when in Milan. It's famous for its vibrant nightlife, cozy cafés, art galleries, and excellent restaurants. Though it's a fantastic place to explore, the noise, crowds, and lengthy waits at bars and restaurants can make a weekend evening visit intimidating.

WHY SHOULD YOU AVOID IT?

On weekends, especially during the evening, Navigli becomes incredibly crowded, with both tourists and locals looking to enjoy aperitivo or a night out. It can be challenging to navigate the narrow streets beside the canals or secure a seat at a restaurant or bar because they fill up quickly. You might find yourself waiting for ages to get a table, and the usually relaxing and scenic atmosphere of Navigli is replaced by a noisy, bustling crowd.

With the large influx of people, the prices at some establishments may also be higher than during weekdays, and service can be slower due to the demand. This confluence of elements may take away from what ought to be a delightful and delightful stroll along Milan's ancient canals.

WHAT TO DO INSTEAD?

- **Visit During the Weekdays:** Visit Navigli during the weekdays to enjoy its charm without the oppressive crowds. The area is much quieter, and you'll have more space to explore the canals, enjoy a peaceful aperitivo, and check out local galleries. The restaurants are less packed, and you're more likely to get a good seat with attentive service.

- **Go During the Daytime:** The Navigli District is also lovely to explore during the day, particularly if you're interested in browsing its many artisan shops and galleries. You can take your time exploring the markets, strolling along the canals, or sipping coffee at a café without the bustle of the evening crowd because there are fewer people around.
- **Consider an Early Aperitivo:** Go earlier in the evening if you still want to take in Navigli's renowned aperitivo scene. Arriving between 5 PM and 7 PM ensures you'll beat the late-night crowd and have a more relaxed experience.

ADDITIONAL TIPS

- **Explore Lesser-Known Canals**: In addition to the main Navigli Grande, explore smaller canals like **Naviglio Pavese**, which are often quieter but still offer great spots for food and drinks.
- **Book a Table in Advance**: Make reservations in advance if you must visit on a weekend night to avoid standing in line at busy bars and restaurants.

By avoiding Navigli on weekend evenings and opting for quieter times, you'll be able to enjoy the district's charm and unique vibe without the hassle of overcrowding and noise.

6. SKIP WAITING IN LINE FOR LAST SUPPER TICKETS

One of Milan's most iconic cultural treasures is Leonardo da Vinci's masterpiece, *The Last Supper*. This famous mural, housed in the **Santa Maria delle Grazie** convent, is a must-see for many visitors. However, entry lines can get very long, especially if you haven't planned ahead, and tickets are limited and sell out quickly.

WHY SHOULD YOU AVOID IT?

Seeing *The Last Supper* without proper preparation can be frustrating. Numerous attendees must wait in lengthy lineups in the hopes of obtaining a spot because tickets frequently sell out months in advance. Even if you do manage to buy a ticket on the day, you could spend hours waiting, only to experience the artwork for a very brief time. Additionally, those who try to book last minute may face disappointment as the limited number of daily visitors is strictly enforced to preserve the artwork.

This has the potential to make an exciting cultural encounter into a stressful one, especially when there are easier ways to ensure your visit without the hassle of long lines or missed opportunities.

WHAT TO DO INSTEAD?

- **Book Tickets Online in Advance:** The best way to avoid long lines and ensure you see *The Last Supper* is to book your tickets well in advance. Tickets are available online and are released up to three months ahead of time. Booking directly through the official website or authorized resellers will secure your spot without the need to queue. To prevent humidity and temperature fluctuations from damaging the fragile mural, a cap on visitor numbers necessitates reservations.

- **Opt for a Guided Tour with Skip-the-Line Access:** Making reservations for a guided tour that offers skip-the-line access is still another fantastic choice. Many tour companies offer packages that combine visits to other important Milanese sites with a timed entry to *The Last Supper*. This not only allows you to bypass the long queues but also gives you a richer experience with commentary from knowledgeable guides.

- **Consider a Package Deal with Other Attractions:** Some tour operators offer combination tickets that include *The Last Supper* along with other attractions like the **Duomo** or **Sforza Castle**. These packages guarantee you make the most of your time in Milan without having to wait in long lines and frequently include skip-the-line access.

ADDITIONAL TIPS

- **Plan Your Visit Early**: Book as soon as you know your travel dates to ensure availability.
- **Check for Last-Minute Cancellations**: If you haven't booked in advance, some resellers offer last-minute tickets, but be prepared to pay a premium.

By making a reservation in advance or taking a guided tour, you'll avoid the long lines and frustration of missing out on *The Last Supper*, ensuring a smooth and memorable visit to this Milanese masterpiece.

7. AVOID SHOPPING IN THE GALLERIA VITTORIO EMANUELE II

The **Galleria Vittorio Emanuele II** is one of Milan's most stunning landmarks, known for its grand architecture and luxury stores. While it's a must-visit for its historical and architectural significance, shopping here can be a different story. Some of the most upscale brands in the world can be found at The Galleria, so although window shopping is fun, making actual purchases in this famous arcade might not be the best use of your money unless you're ready to pay exorbitant prices.

WHY SHOULD YOU AVOID IT?

The stores in the Galleria cater to a luxury clientele, with flagship boutiques for brands like Prada, Louis Vuitton, and Gucci. These stores come with premium prices that are often higher than those found elsewhere in the city. If you're looking for something more affordable or unique, you're unlikely to find it here. Shopping at The Galleria can sometimes feel more like a crowded sightseeing event than a pleasurable retail experience due to its popularity with tourists.

Beyond the luxury brands, many of the shops in the Galleria are global chain stores, meaning you might end up paying Milan prices for items you could buy elsewhere for less.

WHAT TO DO INSTEAD?

- **Shop in Brera or Navigli for Unique Finds:** For a more authentic Milanese shopping experience, head to the **Brera** or **Navigli** districts. Brera is known for its independent boutiques and artisan shops offering one-of-a-kind fashion, jewelry, and accessories. Navigli, with its more relaxed vibe, is a great place to find vintage stores and art galleries that sell unique, locally crafted items at more affordable prices.
- **Visit Corso Buenos Aires for High-Street Fashion:** The place to go if you're searching for high-street fashion at more affordable prices is **Corso Buenos Aires**. This bustling shopping street has a wide range of stores, from Italian brands to international chains, offering a better variety of price points compared to the Galleria.
- **Explore Milan's Outlet Stores:** Milan offers a number of outlets where you can get fantastic discounts on high-end merchandise if you're keen to get designer goods at a lower price. **Serravalle Designer Outlet** and **Il Salvagente** are popular options for shoppers looking for bargains on high-end fashion.

ADDITIONAL TIPS

- **Window Shop for the Experience**: If you do visit the Galleria, enjoy the architecture and atmosphere, but avoid impulse buys unless you're specifically looking for luxury items.
- **Check Local Boutiques for Italian Brands**: Milan is full of independent Italian designers offering unique pieces that reflect the city's fashion-forward culture.

By avoiding shopping in the Galleria Vittorio Emanuele II and exploring other districts, you'll find more affordable, unique, and authentic items while still enjoying Milan's renowned shopping scene.

8. AVOID ATTENDING FASHION WEEK WITHOUT PLANNING

Milan is one of the world's fashion capitals, and **Milan Fashion Week** is one of the most glamorous events on the global fashion calendar. Being present at or close to the action during this prestigious event is a dream come true for many attendees. However, trying to attend Milan Fashion Week without prior planning can lead to disappointment and frustration, as it's not a public event that you can simply walk into.

WHY SHOULD YOU AVOID IT?

The majority of the shows and presentations during Milan Fashion Week are exclusively for industry insiders, celebrities, and buyers. Tickets are generally not available to the public, and access is by invitation only. Many tourists mistakenly believe they can attend the high-profile runway shows, only to find that these events are closed to outsiders. Trying to navigate the city during Fashion Week without a plan can be overwhelming, as the streets around show venues are crowded with paparazzi, influencers, and industry professionals, making it difficult to move around.

Additionally, hotel prices surge during this time, and many restaurants and bars near Fashion Week venues are packed or booked for private events, making it more difficult to enjoy the city.

WHAT TO DO INSTEAD?

- **Attend Public Fashion Events:** Although the main runway shows are exclusive, there are plenty of public events and exhibitions during Milan Fashion Week. Many boutiques and stores host open events, parties, and showcases where you can get a taste of the fashion scene without needing an invite. During Fashion Week, look through your local listings for pop-up stores, street-style gatherings, and exhibitions.
- **Visit During Other Fashion-Related Events:** If you're a fashion enthusiast but can't attend Fashion Week, consider visiting during **Milano Unica** (a fashion textile fair) or **Vogue for Milano** (an event in September

celebrating fashion and shopping). These public gatherings provide an opportunity to interact with Milanese fashion culture without the seclusion of Fashion Week.
- **Shop at Boutiques and Designer Stores:** Make use of the many boutiques and designer stores in the city to get a taste of Milan's fashion scene. Even outside of Fashion Week, Milan's **Quadrilatero della Moda** district is home to the world's most luxurious brands, where you can shop or simply admire the collections.

ADDITIONAL TIPS

- **Plan Accommodations Early:** Make sure to reserve your hotel well in advance if you plan to visit Milan during Fashion Week, as availability and prices tend to change closer to the event dates.
- **Follow Fashion Week Online:** Many designers now livestream their runway shows, so you can still enjoy the spectacle from the comfort of your accommodation.

By avoiding the hectic crowds and exclusivity of Milan Fashion Week without proper planning, you can take in other fashion shows or leisurely stroll through Milan's vibrant fashion district.

9. DON'T OVERPAY FOR APERITIVO IN THE TRENDY ZONES

Aperitivo is an integral part of Milan's culture—a pre-dinner ritual where you enjoy drinks accompanied by small bites or even a buffet of appetizers. It's a well-liked custom that provides a soothing way to wind down following a day of sightseeing. However, in trendy areas like **Brera** and **Corso Como**, aperitivo prices can be steep, and what should be a casual, affordable treat can quickly become overpriced.

WHY SHOULD YOU AVOID IT?

Certain bars in Milan's trendier areas overcharge for aperitivo, especially when serving guests who are visiting. A simple drink that typically comes with complimentary snacks can cost upwards of €15 or more in these hotspots. Many of these places capitalize on their location, offering flashy settings but often skimping on food quality or portions while charging a premium for the experience.

While it's tempting to grab a seat at a trendy bar, you might end up paying much more for your aperitivo than necessary. Furthermore, the bustling nature of these well-liked locations can contribute to a louder, less tranquil experience, which takes away from the informal ambiance of aperitivo.

WHAT TO DO INSTEAD?

- **Explore Local Neighborhoods:** Venture outside of the tourist-heavy zones and explore local neighborhoods like **Porta Romana** or **Isola**, where you can enjoy aperitivo at a fraction of the price found in Brera or Corso Como. Locals prefer to hang out in these more genuine settings, which have copious snacks and reasonably priced drinks.
- **Find Bars with Good Aperitivo Deals:** Great aperitivo deals can be found at several bars in Milan, where you can get a drink and an appetizer buffet for about €8 to €10. Look for places that provide a wide variety of snacks, from **bruschetta** to **cured meats** and cheeses, without charging extra for the setting.
- **Opt for a Simple Aperitivo:** If you're just looking to enjoy a drink and light snacks without the fancy setting, head to smaller, unassuming bars. The aperitivo custom will still be available to you but without the exorbitant costs and hordes of tourists.

ADDITIONAL TIPS

- **Avoid High-Profile Bars:** The more famous or centrally located a bar, the more likely you are to overpay for the experience.
- **Ask Locals for Recommendations:** Locals know the best spots for aperitivo, where you can enjoy a relaxed atmosphere and get more value for your money.

You can take advantage of Milan's aperitivo culture without breaking the bank or having to deal with tourist crowds by eschewing the trendy, expensive aperitivo spots and exploring local, laid-back venues instead.

10. SKIP VISITING CASTELLO SFORZESCO MIDDAY

Castello Sforzesco, a historic fortress in Milan, is a must-see for anyone interested in history, art, and architecture. This magnificent castle is a well-liked attraction because it houses several museums and is surrounded by lovely grounds. However, visiting during midday can make the experience less enjoyable due to the large crowds and heat, especially during the summer months.

WHY SHOULD YOU AVOID IT?

In the middle of the day, especially during the busiest travel seasons, the castle fills up with tour groups, school trips, and people trying to see everything at once. This can lead to long waits to enter the museums, packed hallways, and difficulty fully appreciating the exhibits and art within the castle's museums. The experience can be rushed and less immersive with the crowds.

Moreover, the castle's large outdoor courtyard and gardens can become uncomfortable under the midday sun, especially during the hot Milanese summers. There isn't much shade in some spots, and the heat and crowds can make it less peaceful to stroll through the castle grounds.

WHAT TO DO INSTEAD?

- **Visit Early in the Morning:** When Castello Sforzesco first opens in the morning is the ideal time to visit. You'll avoid the large crowds, enjoy a quieter atmosphere, and have more space to explore both the museums and the outdoor areas. The morning light also makes for better photography, especially around the scenic courtyards and gardens.
- **Opt for a Late Afternoon Visit:** If you can't visit in the morning, think about going in the late afternoon. By this time, many of the tour groups and larger crowds will have moved on, and the heat of the day begins to

cool. The castle is open until the evening, giving you plenty of time to explore at a relaxed pace.
- **Combine Your Visit with Sempione Park**: Castello Sforzesco is adjacent to **Parco Sempione**, one of Milan's largest parks. After your castle visit, take a leisurely stroll through the park, where you'll find shady spots to rest and enjoy the peaceful greenery. This combination provides a relaxing diversion from the city's busier areas.

ADDITIONAL TIPS

- **Buy Tickets in Advance**: Consider purchasing tickets online to avoid waiting in line during busy periods.
- **Check Museum Times**: The various museums inside the castle have different opening hours, so plan your visit accordingly

By avoiding the midday rush and exploring Castello Sforzesco during quieter hours, you'll have a more enjoyable and immersive experience while appreciating one of Milan's most historic sites.

Milan is a city that beautifully balances modernity with tradition, offering visitors a mix of world-class fashion, art, history, and culinary delights. But like any well-known location, there are tourist traps and expensive activities that can detract from the genuine charm of the city. By knowing what to avoid, you can experience Milan like a local, making the most of your time without falling into common pitfalls.

This guide has shown you how to get around Milan wisely, from avoiding crowded hotspots like the Navigli District on weekends to avoiding overpriced shopping in the Galleria Vittorio Emanuele II. Exploring quieter neighborhoods, dining away from the tourist centers, and booking tickets in advance for must-see attractions like *The Last Supper* are just a few of the ways to ensure a more genuine and enjoyable visit.

Milan's real beauty is found in the way it combines history, culture, and daily life. By taking time to wander through local markets, enjoy aperitivo in lesser-known bars, and visit iconic sites during off-peak hours, you'll get to experience the city in a deeper and more meaningful way. Whether you're visiting for the fashion, the art, or just to immerse yourself in its vibrant atmosphere, Milan rewards those who take the road less traveled.

NAPLES

With its rich history, dynamic culture, and lively life, Naples provides visitors with an experience that is unmatched anywhere else in Italy. Known as the birthplace of pizza, home to ancient ruins like Pompeii, and boasting views of the iconic Mount Vesuvius, Naples has something to offer every type of visitor. The city's historic center, a UNESCO World Heritage Site, is filled with narrow streets, bustling markets, and a lively atmosphere that reflects the energy of its people.

Even though Naples has a lot to offer, it also has its share of difficulties. From chaotic traffic and crowded public transportation to occasional safety concerns, there are some aspects of the city that travelers should be aware of to ensure they have a smooth and enjoyable visit. Whether it's avoiding overpriced restaurants near tourist hotspots or knowing when and where to explore, a little preparation can go a long way in getting the most out of your trip to Naples.

This guide outlines the top ten things you should not do while visiting Naples in order to avoid typical tourist traps and fully appreciate the genuine essence of the city. By navigating these potential challenges, you'll be able to enjoy the best of what Naples has to offer—its food, history, and undeniable charm—without unnecessary stress.

1. AVOID DRIVING IN THE CITY

Naples is a city known for its energetic atmosphere and bustling streets, and nowhere is this more evident than in its chaotic traffic. While renting a car may seem like a convenient option for getting around, driving in Naples is something most tourists should avoid. The city's winding streets, dense traffic, and erratic driving can make for an unpleasant journey instead of a fun one.

WHY SHOULD YOU AVOID IT?

Driving in Naples is not for the faint of heart. Those who are not familiar with the city may find it challenging to navigate the streets because they are frequently winding and narrow. Neapolitan drivers are known for their aggressive style, frequently disregarding traffic rules and honking, which is a constant sound in the city. Traffic congestion is a common issue, especially in the historic center, and parking is extremely limited, often leading to frustration. Even if you do find parking, it can be expensive, and your car may not always be in the safest area.

- Additionally, Naples has many **Zona a Traffico Limitato (ZTL)** areas, restricted traffic zones where driving is only permitted for residents or authorized vehicles. Due to a lack of signage, visitors who unintentionally drive into these zones may be subject to severe fines.

WHAT TO DO INSTEAD?

- **Use Public Transportation:** Buses, trams, and a metro network are all part of Naples' dependable and reasonably priced public transportation network. The metro system, particularly lines 1 and 2, connects most major attractions, and the **Funicolare** (cable cars) can take you up to scenic viewpoints like **Vomero**. Public transport is easy to navigate and much less stressful than driving.
- **Take Taxis or Ride-Sharing Services:** If you prefer a more direct mode of transport, taxis and ride-sharing apps like **mytaxi** are readily available in Naples. Be sure to use licensed taxis, as unlicensed ones can overcharge. Using official taxis is a convenient way to move around without having to deal with traffic.
- **Walk Through the Historic Center:** Many of Naples' most famous attractions, like **Spaccanapoli**, the **Duomo**, and the **Archaeological Museum**, are located within walking distance of each other. You can get a close-up look at the city's charm by strolling through the historic center

without having to worry about driving.

ADDITIONAL TIPS

- **Avoid Renting a Car**: If you're planning day trips outside of Naples, consider taking the train instead of driving. Trains travel frequently and provide easy access to destinations such as Pompeii, Sorrento, and the Amalfi Coast.

By avoiding the stress of driving in Naples and opting for public transport, taxis, or walking, you'll enjoy a much smoother and more enjoyable visit to the city.

2. SKIP TOURIST RESTAURANTS NEAR MAJOR LANDMARKS

Naples is well-known for its amazing food, especially its pizza, which is regarded as some of the greatest in the world. However, when dining near major landmarks such as **Piazza del Plebiscito, Castel dell'Ovo**, or along the waterfront, you're likely to encounter restaurants that cater mainly to tourists, offering overpriced meals and subpar versions of local dishes.

WHY SHOULD YOU AVOID IT?

Restaurants around popular tourist spots often focus more on convenience and location than on food quality. These eateries tend to have inflated prices, with dishes costing significantly more than in less tourist-heavy areas, and the food often lacks the authenticity you'd expect from Naples. It's possible to find bland renditions of classic Neapolitan cuisine that fall short of the city's gastronomic reputation.

In addition to overpriced meals, service can sometimes be less attentive in these tourist-oriented restaurants. High foot traffic means they rely on a constant stream of new visitors rather than repeat customers, leading to a more generic dining experience that lacks the charm and warmth of smaller, family-run trattorias.

WHAT TO DO INSTEAD?

- **Explore Neighborhoods Like Vomero and Chiaia:** Venture beyond the tourist zones and explore neighborhoods like **Vomero** and **Chiaia**, where locals dine. Here, you'll find authentic Neapolitan cuisine at much more reasonable prices. These neighborhoods are well-known for their classic pizzerias and trattorias that serve food prepared using local, fresh ingredients.
- **Ask Locals for Recommendations:** Neapolitans are proud of their cuisine and frequently enjoy showing off their best restaurants. Ask a local for a restaurant recommendation, and you'll likely be directed to a hidden gem serving authentic Neapolitan cuisine.
- **Look for Pizzerias Off the Beaten Path:** For a true Neapolitan pizza experience, avoid the tourist traps and head to famous yet affordable pizzerias like **Pizzeria Sorbillo** or **Di Matteo**. These places are well-known for their authentic, tasty pizza that is reasonably priced and free of tourist markup.

ADDITIONAL TIPS

- **Avoid Menus in Multiple Languages:** Restaurants offering menus in several languages often cater to tourists and may lack authenticity. Look for restaurants with a predominantly Italian menu; this suggests a more local clientele.
- **Check the Reviews:** A quick look at online reviews can help you avoid overpriced tourist spots and find places with genuine local flavor.

By skipping the touristy restaurants near major landmarks and exploring less tourist-heavy areas, you'll enjoy a more authentic, flavorful, and affordable dining experience in Naples.

3. DON'T TAKE UNOFFICIAL TAXIS

Although using an unofficial or unlicensed taxi can be risky, they are a convenient way to get around Naples, especially for visitors who are not familiar with the public transportation system. These vehicles are often found near popular areas like the **Central Station** or **Naples International Airport**, and while they may seem like an easy option, they can lead to overpriced rides and other potential problems.

WHY SHOULD YOU AVOID IT?

Unofficial taxis, or "black cabs," don't follow regulated fare structures, meaning you could end up paying far more than a typical ride. Many tourists have reported being charged exorbitant rates, particularly from drivers targeting first-time visitors unfamiliar with local prices. These drivers frequently operate without the required license, which can make it challenging to resolve any problems that may arise, like disputes over routes or overcharging.

Additionally, safety can be a concern with unofficial taxis. While most drivers are just trying to make a living, you're still taking a risk by getting into a vehicle that isn't regulated or monitored by local authorities.

WHAT TO DO INSTEAD?

- **Use Official Taxis:** Official taxis in Naples are easy to identify. They are white with a taxi sign on the roof and display a license number on the doors. These taxis operate under a regulated fare system, and many now offer fixed rates for common routes, like trips to and from the airport or train stations. To avoid any confusion, always request a receipt at the conclusion of the trip.
- **Use Ride-Hailing Apps:** Ride-hailing services like **mytaxi** or **Free Now** (formerly known as Hailo) are available in Naples and provide a safe, transparent way to book a ride. With the ability to pay through the app, you can avoid the possibility of being overcharged. These apps also display estimated fares and track your journey in real time.
- **Agree on a Price in Advance:** If you do decide to take a taxi, especially for a longer journey, it's a good idea to agree on the price beforehand. This can help avoid any misunderstandings or inflated fares at the end of the

trip. Ask to see the fixed price list for popular destinations that official taxis frequently have.

ADDITIONAL TIPS

- **Check the Meter**: Always ensure the meter is running when you enter an official taxi. If the driver refuses or tries to negotiate a high fare without using the meter, it's better to find another taxi.
- **Stick to Licensed Drivers**: Avoid any driver who approaches you offering a ride, particularly close to crowded locations like the airport or train station. Seek for licensed taxis that are properly marked.

By avoiding unofficial taxis and opting for regulated, licensed drivers or ride-hailing apps, you'll ensure a safer, more cost-effective journey through Naples.

4. AVOID THE OVERCROWDED CIRCUMVESUVIANA TRAIN AT PEAK TIMES

The **Circumvesuviana** train is a popular way to travel from Naples to nearby attractions like **Pompeii**, **Herculaneum**, and **Sorrento**. While the train can get very crowded during peak hours, making for an uncomfortable and less enjoyable travel experience, it is still a convenient option, particularly for day trips.

WHY SHOULD YOU AVOID IT?

The Circumvesuviana train, while affordable, is notorious for being overcrowded during peak hours, particularly in the summer months when tourists flock to Pompeii and the Amalfi Coast. Tourists and locals alike frequently cram the trains with people, making it usual to spend the entire trip standing in cramped quarters. There is also no air conditioning on many of these trains, which can make the ride unbearable in the sweltering heat.

Pickpocketing is also a concern on crowded Circumvesuviana trains, as tourists, distracted by the tight spaces and their travel plans, can become easy targets.

What should be a straightforward journey can become extremely stressful before you even arrive at your destination due to delays and limited seating.

WHAT TO DO INSTEAD?

- **Travel Early in the Morning or Late Afternoon:** Plan your trip for early in the morning or late in the afternoon to avoid the Circumvesuviana's busiest periods. This way, you'll avoid the mid-morning and early afternoon rush when tourists and locals pack the train. Traveling at these times increases your chances of getting a seat and having a more comfortable ride.
- **Consider the Campania Express:** The **Campania Express** is a more comfortable alternative to the Circumvesuviana, catering specifically to tourists. It offers air-conditioned carriages, reserved seating, and fewer stops, which means a faster, more enjoyable ride to popular destinations like Pompeii and Sorrento. For a more leisurely ride, the Campania Express is well worth the additional expense, even though it is more expensive than the Circumvesuviana.
- **Opt for a Guided Tour:** If you're heading to Pompeii or Herculaneum, consider booking a guided tour that includes transportation. Many tour companies provide air-conditioned buses that depart from Naples, which include the cost of entry to the sites. By doing this, you can visit historical sites with greater understanding and without the need for public transportation.

ADDITIONAL TIPS

- **Buy Your Tickets in Advance**: Purchasing train tickets in advance, especially for peak travel times, ensure that you won't be stuck in long lines at the station.
- **Keep Valuables Secure**: Always keep an eye on your belongings in crowded spaces, and consider using a money belt or cross-body bag to prevent pickpocketing.

By avoiding the Circumvesuviana during peak times and exploring alternative options like the Campania Express or a guided tour, you can ensure a more comfortable and stress-free journey to Naples' most famous sites.

5. DON'T WANDER ALONE AT NIGHT IN CERTAIN AREAS

Naples is a vibrant and exciting city, but like many major urban areas, there are certain neighborhoods that are best avoided at night, especially if you are unfamiliar with the city or traveling alone. Although Naples is relatively safe overall, there are certain areas with higher than average rates of small-time crimes, so exercise caution, especially after dark.

WHY SHOULD YOU AVOID IT?

- Certain areas in Naples, such as the vicinity around the **Central Station (Napoli Centrale)** and parts of the **Spanish Quarters (Quartieri Spagnoli)**, can be less safe at night. These neighborhoods can have higher crime rates, including pickpocketing and muggings. While many residents go through these areas without any problems, visitors who are not familiar with the city may feel more at risk.

Particularly in less touristy areas, walking alone on dimly lit or empty streets can make you more likely to run into trouble. While serious crime is rare, petty theft and scams are more common, particularly in areas where tourists tend to congregate. Wandering into quieter areas of the city at night, especially without a clear sense of direction, can be unsettling and may lead to uncomfortable situations.

WHAT TO DO INSTEAD?

- **Stick to Well-Lit and Populated Areas:** If you're exploring Naples in the evening, stick to well-lit, busy areas such as **Via Toledo, Piazza Bellini**, or the popular neighborhoods of **Chiaia** and **Vomero**. It is safer to stroll through these areas at night because they are crowded with residents and visitors taking advantage of the exciting nightlife.
- **Travel in Groups or with a Companion:** Traveling with a group or a companion is one of the best ways to stay safe when exploring Naples after

dark. You'll feel more secure and less likely to attract unwanted attention. It's usually a good idea to stick with people if you're out late, especially in new places.
- **Use Taxis or Ride-Sharing Services:** Instead of walking back to your hotel or through quieter areas at night, opt for a taxi or use a ride-sharing app like **taxi**. After dark, licensed taxis offer a safer and more secure means of transportation throughout the city. Refrain from accepting rides from unlicensed drivers who could overcharge or endanger your safety.

ADDITIONAL TIPS

- **Research Your Neighborhood**: Before booking accommodations, research the neighborhood to ensure it's in a safe and well-connected part of the city, particularly if you plan on walking around at night.
- **Keep Valuables Hidden**: If you are out at night, avoid displaying valuables like phones, jewelry, or large amounts of cash to minimize the risk of becoming a target.

By walking only in populated areas at night and exercising caution, well-lit areas or using safe transport options, you'll enjoy a more secure and comfortable stay in Naples.

6. AVOID EATING PIZZA ANYWHERE BUT PIZZERIAS

Pizza originated in Naples, and it's not hyperbole to suggest that this city produces some of the best pizza in the entire globe. However, not all pizza in Naples lives up to its world-class reputation, especially if you grab a slice from a random café, tourist restaurant, or convenience store. To truly experience authentic Neapolitan pizza, it's essential to know where to go and what to avoid.

WHY SHOULD YOU AVOID IT?

Even though pizza is served everywhere in Naples, not all restaurants provide a genuine Neapolitan experience. Many tourist restaurants near popular landmarks serve watered-down, generic versions of pizza that lack the quality, flavor, and authenticity that Naples is famous for. These places often cater to tourists who don't know better, and as a result, the pizza can be overpriced and disappointing.

Moreover, many cafés or snack bars sell reheated pizza slices that have been sitting out for hours, lacking the fresh ingredients and wood-fired oven technique that makes authentic Neapolitan pizza so special. These restaurants' pizzas won't truly capture the essence of Naples' extensive culinary heritage.

WHAT TO DO INSTEAD?

- **Head to Renowned Pizzerias:** Naples is home to some of the most famous pizzerias in the world, such as **L'Antica Pizzeria da Michele** and **Pizzeria Sorbillo**. These iconic spots serve up simple but perfected versions of classic Neapolitan pizza, such as **Margherita** and **Marinara**. These pizzerias are renowned for their use of premium ingredients, slow-rising dough, and authentic wood-fired ovens, all of which combine to create a truly remarkable pizza experience.

- **Look for Local, Family-Run Pizzerias:** You can find excellent pizza anywhere; you're not limited to the most well-known eateries. Many smaller, family-run establishments scattered throughout Naples offer equally delicious, authentic pizza at more reasonable prices. Look for spots that are busy with locals, as these are often the hidden gems serving some of the city's best pizza.

- **Order the Classics:** When eating pizza in Naples, it's best to stick with the traditional options like **Margherita** or **Marinara**. These simple pizzas, made with fresh tomatoes, mozzarella, basil, and olive oil, showcase the quality of the ingredients and the skill of the pizzaiolo (pizza maker). Steer clear of "tourist" or extremely complicated pizzas that might have a lot of extra toppings.

ADDITIONAL TIPS

- **Expect to Wait:** At popular pizzerias like Da Michele or Sorbillo, lines can be long, but the wait is well worth it for the quality of pizza you'll get.

- **Be Prepared for a Simpler Experience**: Authentic Neapolitan pizzerias often focus solely on pizza, with limited drink options and simple menus. Not variety, but quality is the main focus.

By avoiding generic pizza in touristy spots and seeking out Naples' renowned pizzerias, you'll get to experience the true flavor of Neapolitan pizza in all its glory.

7. DON'T FORGET TO VALIDATE YOUR TRAIN OR BUS TICKET

When traveling around Naples via public transportation—whether it's on the **metro, bus,** or **train**—one of the most important things to remember is to validate your ticket before you start your journey. Even though you have a valid ticket, failing to do so may result in significant fines.

WHY SHOULD YOU AVOID IT?

In Naples, simply purchasing a ticket is not enough; you need to validate it before boarding. Your ticket must be stamped at a validation machine to have the date and time stamped on it. If you don't do this, the ticket is considered invalid, and you may face a fine from ticket inspectors, even though you have already paid for your fare. Inspectors frequently check tickets on public transportation, and the fines can be steep, often costing more than €50 on the spot.

For tourists unfamiliar with this system, it's easy to forget or not realize that validation is required. But ticket inspectors aren't forgiving, and you can't avoid paying a fine by claiming ignorance. The validation machines are often located at the entrance to metro stations or inside buses and trains, and they're easy to use—just insert your ticket into the machine until it clicks or stamps.

WHAT TO DO INSTEAD?

- **Always Validate Your Ticket:** Make it a habit to validate your ticket at one of the yellow or orange machines as soon as you get on a bus, enter a metro station, or arrive at a train station. This applies to single-ride tickets, day passes, and multi-day passes. On buses, validation machines are located near the doors, while in metro stations, they're typically at the turnstiles.

- **Check for Validation on Long-Distance Trains:** If you're traveling on regional or long-distance trains, like the **Circumvesuviana,** or trains to Pompeii or Sorrento, you'll need to validate your ticket at the platform before boarding. Since tickets are typically checked on board high-speed trains like **Frecciarossa** and **Italo,** ticket validation may not be necessary, but make sure to check before you travel.

- **Use Mobile Tickets or Contactless Cards:** These days, a lot of Naples transportation services allow users to use contactless payment cards or mobile ticketing. If you use a mobile ticket through an app, the ticket is usually automatically validated when scanned, reducing the risk of forgetting.

ADDITIONAL TIPS

- **Keep Your Ticket Handy:** Even after you validate it, keep your ticket with you for the duration of your journey in case inspectors ask to see it.
- **Watch for the Validation Machines:** Validation machines may vary in color (yellow or orange) and are often placed at entry points of metro stations or on board buses and trains.

By keeping in mind to check your ticket before leaving, you'll avoid unnecessary fines and enjoy a smooth and stress-free experience while exploring Naples by public transportation.

8. SKIP THE WATERFRONT SOUVENIR SHOPS

Naples' stunning waterfront, particularly near **Castel dell'Ovo** and the **Lungomare,** is one of the city's most picturesque areas, drawing tourists with its scenic views and historic sites. Along the waterfront, you'll find rows of souvenir shops, tempting visitors with colorful trinkets, magnets, and "authentic" Neapolitan keepsakes. But these stores are frequently overpriced and stocked with mass-produced goods that don't accurately capture Naples' genuine craftsmanship.

WHY SHOULD YOU AVOID IT?

The souvenir shops along the waterfront are designed to cater to the high volume of tourists, and as a result, the prices for items are often significantly inflated. Most of the goods you'll find—like keychains, postcards, T-shirts, and cheaply made ceramics—are not actually made in Naples or even Italy. These mass-produced goods are less distinctive and intimate because they can be found in other tourist destinations across the globe.

Additionally, the quality of these souvenirs is generally low, meaning that items may break or wear down quickly after purchase. Purchasing from these stores not only results in overspending but also forfeits the chance to bring home a genuinely unique piece of Naples.

WHAT TO DO INSTEAD?

- **Visit Local Artisan Shops:** Naples is known for its craftsmanship, particularly in ceramics, jewelry, and nativity figurines (known as **present**). For a more authentic souvenir, seek out local artisan shops in areas like **Spaccanapoli** or the **Vomero** district. These stores provide locally made goods made by artisans, so you can bring home a one-of-a-kind, fine memento.
- **Explore Naples' Markets:** Another great alternative to waterfront souvenir shops is visiting Naples' lively markets, such as **Pignasecca Market** or **Mercato di Antignano**. Everything from locally produced fresh produce to handcrafted goods can be found here. The prices in these markets are usually far more reasonable than in tourist-heavy areas, and they provide a more genuine shopping experience.
- **Look for Locally Made Products:** When shopping for souvenirs, look for items labeled **Made in Italy** or, better yet, **Made in Naples**. This ensures you're supporting local artisans and taking home something that genuinely reflects the culture and craftsmanship of the region.

ADDITIONAL TIPS

- **Bargain Wisely**: If you're shopping at markets, don't be afraid to negotiate. Though bargaining is customary in the markets of Naples, it isn't always appropriate in upscale stores.
- **Support Small Businesses**: By shopping at local artisan shops and markets, you'll not only get a more meaningful souvenir but also support small businesses that rely on tourism.

By avoiding the overpriced, mass-produced items sold in waterfront souvenir shops and seeking out authentic, locally made goods, you'll bring home a true piece of Naples' culture and craftsmanship.

9. AVOID VISITING MUSEUMS OR ATTRACTIONS ON SUNDAYS WITHOUT A PLAN

Naples is home to incredible museums and historic attractions, such as the **National Archaeological Museum, Capodimonte Museum, and Castel dell'Ovo**. While visiting these sites is a must for any trip to the city, Sundays—especially the first Sunday of each month—can present challenges if you're unprepared. There will be long lines and crowds because many of the state-run museums and attractions in Naples are free to enter on this particular day.

WHY SHOULD YOU AVOID IT?

Free museum admission sounds good, but Sundays—especially the first Sunday of the month—can draw large numbers of visitors and residents alike. The influx of visitors makes it difficult to enjoy the exhibits or fully appreciate the historical significance of the sites. Long queues, packed galleries, and limited space can turn what should be a rich cultural experience into a frustrating ordeal.

In addition, museums may impose time limits on your visit or limit your access to specific areas of the exhibitions because of the large volume of visitors, which would lower the quality of your experience. Even outside of the free admission days, Sundays tend to be busy, with museums and attractions becoming more crowded as both tourists and local families take advantage of their day off.

WHAT TO DO INSTEAD?

- **Visit on a Weekday:** For a more relaxed experience, try visiting museums and major attractions during the week, preferably on a Tuesday or Wednesday, when crowds are typically lighter. It will be more pleasant overall, and you'll have more room to explore at your own pace without the hustle and bustle of big crowds.
- **Arrive Early or Late in the Day:** If you must go on a Sunday, schedule your arrival for either the museum's early morning hours or later in the afternoon, closer to when it closes. Arriving early allows you to beat the rush and enjoy a quieter visit before the crowds descend. Similarly, later in the day, the crowd may start to thin, offering a more peaceful experience.
- **Pre-Book Tickets and Tours:** Even if you're visiting on a free-entry day, consider booking a guided tour or reserving tickets in advance for any paid exhibitions. Some museums let people who have reserved ahead of time get priority access, so you can avoid the lines and get the most out of your visit.

ADDITIONAL TIPS

- **Check for Closures:** Be aware that some museums may have altered hours or may be closed on certain holidays or Sundays, so always check ahead.
- **Use Off-Peak Hours:** If you wish to completely avoid the crowds, plan your visit during off-peak hours, typically mid-morning or later in the afternoon.

By avoiding museums on busy Sundays or planning your visit with careful timing, you'll have a more rewarding and enjoyable cultural experience in Naples.

10. DON'T NEGLECT PERSONAL BELONGINGS IN CROWDED AREAS

Naples is a bustling, energetic city, but like many popular tourist locations, it experiences its fair share of pickpocketing and small-time theft, especially in crowded areas. Whether you're walking through the bustling streets of **Via Toledo**, exploring the **Historic Center**, or passing through **Naples Central Station**, it's essential to be mindful of your belongings to avoid any unpleasant surprises.

WHY SHOULD YOU AVOID IT?

Pickpocketing can occur in any crowded area, and Naples is no exception. Popular tourist spots, public transportation hubs, and busy markets tend to attract opportunistic thieves who target distracted travelers. Losing your wallet, phone, or important documents can quickly ruin an otherwise enjoyable trip. It can be simple for pickpockets to go unnoticed in the bustle of the city, with congested buses, busy streets, and general hustle and bustle.

Tourists are often easy targets, especially if they're visibly carrying valuable items or aren't paying close attention to their surroundings. Losing possessions can happen even from a momentary lack of attention, so it's critical to take preventative measures to stay safe.

WHAT TO DO INSTEAD?

- **Use Anti-Theft Bags:** Invest in an anti-theft bag, preferably one that has slash-resistant straps, locking zippers, and RFID-blocking technology to protect your personal information. Wearing a cross-body bag in front of you makes it more difficult for pickpockets to get to your possessions and lets you keep a closer check on them.
- **Keep Valuables Out of Reach:** Never store valuable items like your phone, wallet, or passport in easily accessible places such as back pockets or open bags. Instead, use inside pockets or money belts that are harder for thieves to reach. In crowded places, think about wearing your

backpack in front of you or opt for a compact, safe daypack instead.
- **Be Aware of Your Surroundings:** Stay alert when you're in busy places like train stations, markets, or crowded attractions. Pickpockets often work in groups and may try to distract you while someone else steals from you. Stealing can be discouraged by being aware of your surroundings and exercising caution.

ADDITIONAL TIPS

- **Avoid Flashing Valuables:** Try not to openly display expensive items like jewelry, high-end cameras, or large amounts of cash, which can make you a target for theft.
- **Keep a Photocopy of Important Documents:** In case of theft, having a photocopy of your passport and other important documents can be helpful for reporting and replacing them.

By taking these precautions and staying vigilant, you can enjoy Naples without worrying about losing your belongings in crowded areas. A little planning ahead will help to ensure a smooth and safe journey.

Visitors will have an amazing time in Naples, a city brimming with energy, culture, and history. But like any popular destination, it has its share of difficulties and tourist traps. By knowing what to avoid—from navigating its chaotic traffic to steering clear of overpriced tourist traps—you can discover the true heart of this incredible city.

By following this guide, you'll bypass the typical tourist mistakes and experience Naples in its most authentic form. Whether it's dining in local pizzerias, staying safe in crowded areas, or navigating public transportation, these tips will help you enjoy Naples more like a local. You can enjoy the city's exciting street life, top-notch dining options, and wealth of historical treasures without needless stress with a little preparation and awareness.

Naples rewards those who explore it thoughtfully, and by avoiding the common missteps, your time in this captivating city will be filled with discovery, flavor, and adventure. You'll leave Naples with priceless memories of this well-known Italian treasure if you take in its charm while avoiding the crowds.

VERONA

Verona, often overshadowed by nearby Venice and Milan, is a captivating city known for its rich history, stunning architecture, and romantic associations with Shakespeare's *Romeo and Juliet*. Verona is a city where history and culture coexist peacefully, from the historic Arena, where operas fill the night air, to the charming cafés and picturesque streets.

However, like many popular destinations, Verona comes with its share of tourist traps and common pitfalls. The crowds at Juliet's Balcony, overpriced restaurants near major landmarks, and unexpected restrictions in the historic center can sometimes detract from the city's beauty. You can experience Verona more authentically and without the usual tourist annoyances if you know what to avoid.

We'll go over ten must-avoid items in this guide to make your trip to Verona easier and more pleasurable. By steering clear of the crowds, scams, and unnecessary expenses, you'll be able to immerse yourself fully in the charm and magic of this timeless city.

1. AVOID VISITING JULIET'S BALCONY AT PEAK HOURS

Juliet's Balcony, one of Verona's most famous landmarks, draws countless visitors each year, all eager to see the site connected to Shakespeare's *Romeo and Juliet*. Even though many people consider it a must-see, going during busy times can result in crowds, lengthy lines, and a less pleasurable experience all around.

WHY SHOULD YOU AVOID IT?

The small courtyard beneath Juliet's Balcony often becomes packed with tourists, especially during midday and early afternoon. Navigating through the crowds can be difficult, and taking photos of the balcony without a sea of people in the background can feel impossible. The romantic ambiance that visitors anticipate when visiting this famous location is also diminished by the clamor and noise. Moreover, waiting in line to stand on the balcony can take time that could be spent exploring other beautiful parts of the city.

It is also more difficult to take in the space at your own pace because tour groups frequently encircle the balcony area. It's common for visitors to feel rushed or pressured by the sheer volume of people trying to have their own "Romeo and Juliet" moment.

WHAT TO DO INSTEAD?

- **Visit Early in the Morning or Late in the Evening:** To avoid the crowds, plan your visit early in the morning or late in the evening. These times are much quieter, and you'll have a better chance of experiencing the courtyard with fewer people. You can enjoy the setting and take in the surroundings because of the calm atmosphere.
- **Admire from Afar:** Even if you would rather avoid the throngs of people and lengthy lineups, you can still enjoy Juliet's Balcony from a distance. You'll be able to take photos of the balcony and the statue of Juliet without having to wait in line or navigate through a packed courtyard.
- **Explore Other Romeo and Juliet Landmarks:** Verona is full of sites that were inspired by Romeo and Juliet, including **Juliet's Tomb** and **Romeo's House**, which tend to be less crowded than the balcony but still offer interesting insights into the city's literary connections.

ADDITIONAL TIPS

- **Skip the Balcony Climb**: It might sound romantic to stand on the balcony, but it's often not worth the long wait. Simply admiring it from below is just as memorable.
- **Combine with Nearby Attractions**: Juliet's Balcony is located in Verona's historic center, so it would be simple to incorporate a tour of the Verona

Arena or a stroll around Piazza delle Erbe with your visit.

By going during off-peak hours and selecting slower periods to visit, you'll enjoy a more peaceful experience at Juliet's Balcony, allowing the romantic charm of Verona to shine through.

2. SKIP DINING NEAR PIAZZA DELLE ERBE

Piazza delle Erbe is one of Verona's most beautiful squares, filled with historical buildings, statues, and a lively market atmosphere. It's a great spot to visit and soak in the city's charm, but when it comes to dining, the restaurants surrounding the piazza are best avoided. A lot of these places serve mostly tourists and serve subpar food at exorbitant costs.

WHY SHOULD YOU AVOID IT?

The restaurants and cafés around Piazza delle Erbe tend to charge higher prices due to their prime location. While the views of the square are stunning, the food is often average at best, and portions can be smaller than expected. Rather than serving genuine Veronese food, these eateries frequently prioritize customer convenience.

Additionally, the menus are often designed to appeal to an international audience, with dishes that are less representative of true local flavors. Verona is renowned for its vibrant and rich cuisine, but you might find more generic options that don't have the same authenticity as traditional Italian food.

WHAT TO DO INSTEAD?

- **Venture into Side Streets for Authentic Trattorias:** Just a short walk away from Piazza delle Erbe, you'll find smaller, family-run trattorias that offer delicious, authentic Veronese dishes at more reasonable prices. You can often find hidden gems where the food is prepared with care and the atmosphere feels more local by exploring the side streets that lead away from the tourist attractions.
- **Explore Neighborhoods Like San Zeno:** The **San Zeno** neighborhood is

known for its traditional restaurants serving dishes like **risotto all'Amarone** (a rich risotto made with local Amarone wine) and **pastissada de caval** (a traditional Veronese stew). You can have a more genuine dining experience here without having to pay tourist rates.
- **Ask Locals for Recommendations:** Locals in Verona take great pride in their cuisine, and they'll often be happy to point you to their favorite spots away from the main tourist areas. You can find some of the best meals in the city, where quality and price are much more balanced, by asking for a recommendation.

ADDITIONAL TIPS

- **Check Menus Carefully**: If you find yourself near Piazza delle Erbe, take a look at the menus and compare prices. If the menu is overly tourist-friendly with many non-local dishes,It's advisable to search further.
- **Try Local Specialties**: Don't miss out on traditional Veronese dishes like **bigoli** (a thick, spaghetti-like pasta) or **bollito misto** (a mix of boiled meats served with sauces), which are frequently found in eateries that are more genuine.

By avoiding the overpriced restaurants around Piazza delle Erbe and exploring Verona's hidden culinary gems, You'll have a more fulfilling and real dining experience.

3. DON'T DRIVE IN THE HISTORIC CENTER

Verona's historic center is a maze of narrow, cobblestone streets that exude charm and history at every corner. However, driving through this area can be a frustrating and costly mistake for visitors. There are numerous restricted zones where only residents or authorized vehicles are permitted, and the majority of the city center is pedestrianized.

WHY SHOULD YOU AVOID IT?

- Driving in Verona's historic center is not only difficult but also highly restricted. Much of the area is designated as a **Zona a Traffico Limitato**

(ZTL), meaning that only vehicles with special permits are allowed. You risk paying steep fines if you inadvertently enter one of these zones. ZTL signs are often hard to spot, and tourists unfamiliar with the rules can easily get caught out.

Additionally, the streets in the historic center are narrow, making driving stressful, especially for those not used to navigating tight spaces. Additionally, there is extremely little parking, and what little is available is usually expensive. Even if you manage to find parking, the cost and inconvenience of getting in and out of the city center are rarely worth it.

WHAT TO DO INSTEAD?

- **Walk or Use Public Transportation:** Verona is a compact and walkable city, especially in the historic center. Most major attractions, such as the **Arena di Verona, Piazza delle Erbe,** and **Juliet's Balcony,** are within easy walking distance of each other. Strolling spares you the trouble of negotiating congested streets and lets you take in the beauty of the city at your own pace.
- **Use Public Transport or Taxis:** The public transportation in Verona is reasonably priced and operates effectively for longer trips. Buses can take you to areas outside the city center, and taxis are available for quicker, more direct routes. Both options are far more practical than driving and offer a much more relaxing way to see the city.
- **Park Outside the Center:** It is advisable to park in a designated lot outside the historic center if you are traveling outside of Verona with a rented car. You can enter the city from there by bus or walking. Parking garages like **Parcheggio Cittadella** or **Parcheggio Arena** are convenient options that allow you to leave your car safely while you explore the city on foot.

ADDITIONAL TIPS

- **Check for ZTL Zones:** If you must drive through Verona, be sure to check a map of the city's ZTL zones to avoid costly fines.
- **Rent a Bike:** There are bike rentals in Verona, which are a great alternative

to driving and allow you to explore the city more freely while avoiding the traffic.

You'll enjoy touring the city's historic sites much more if you forgo the hassle of driving through Verona's historic center and instead use more practical transportation options.

4. AVOID TAKING A GONDOLA RIDE ON THE ADIGE RIVER

While gondola rides are iconic in Venice, you might be tempted to experience a similar attraction in Verona along the **Adige River**. Taking a gondola ride in Verona can be disappointing and expensive despite the romantic idea of floating along the picturesque waterway.

WHY SHOULD YOU AVOID IT?

Gondola rides on the Adige River in Verona are more of a tourist trap than a major feature of the city's identity, in contrast to Venice. The riverbanks in Verona are not as picturesque as the canals of Venice, and the experience often feels less authentic. Gondola operators in Verona tend to cater mainly to tourists, offering short rides at inflated prices without the charm that one would expect from such an activity.

Given that the majority of Verona's top attractions are situated far from the riverbanks in the historic center, the ride itself doesn't provide many particularly memorable views or experiences. In addition, depending on the time of year, the river's water levels can fluctuate, making the ride less smooth and pleasant.

WHAT TO DO INSTEAD?

- **Walk Along the Adige River:** Instead of paying for a gondola ride, take a stroll along the **Lungadige**—the scenic pathways that run alongside the river. From here, you'll enjoy lovely views of Verona's bridges, such as **Ponte Pietra**, and take in the city's beautiful architecture without spending a dime. It's a tranquil way to take your time discovering the city.

- **Cross Verona's Historic Bridges:** Verona's bridges, including **Ponte Scaligero** and **Ponte Pietra**, are iconic in their own right and offer fantastic views of the city and the river. Without taking a boat ride, you can get a fantastic view of the river and the skyline of Verona by walking across these bridges.
- **Take a City Tour Instead:** Instead of taking a gondola ride, think about doing a guided city tour if you want a more immersive experience. Walking tours or bike tours of Verona's historic sites will give you a deeper understanding of the city's history and culture while ensuring you don't miss its most important landmarks.

ADDITIONAL TIPS

- **Visit Castel San Pietro**: For breathtaking views of the Adige River and Verona's historic center, hike or take the funicular to **Castel San Pietro**. Nothing compares to the unparalleled view from the summit, and is certainly worth the short gondola ride.
- **Enjoy a Sunset Walk**: The river is especially lovely at dusk, making it a perfect time for a relaxing stroll along the Lungadige.

By avoiding the gondola rides on the Adige River, which are both expensive and disappointing, you'll have more time to explore the best that Verona has to offer on foot, taking in the city's stunning architecture and scenic views from its historic bridges.

5. SKIP THE JULIET STATUE TRADITION

The statue of Juliet, located beneath her famous balcony at **Casa di Giulietta**, is one of the most popular tourist attractions in Verona. Many visitors flock to the site to take pictures and rub the statue's right breast for good luck in love. But rather than being a true cultural practice, this tradition is more of a modern tourist gimmick, so it's worth giving it another look.

WHY SHOULD YOU AVOID IT?

The custom of rubbing statues has no literary or historical roots; it's a purely modern invention created to cater to tourists. Rubbing Juliet's statue has little to do with Verona's rich history or Shakespeare's play, and participating in the tradition can feel a bit forced, especially considering the large crowds that gather around the statue at all times of the day.

Furthermore, over time, the statue has sustained significant wear and damage due to frequent touching. The original bronze statue suffered so much from this tradition that it was eventually moved to a museum and replaced by a replica. While it may seem like a fun photo opportunity, the practice doesn't add much value to your experience in Verona.

WHAT TO DO INSTEAD?

- **Visit Juliet's Balcony Early or Late:** While the statue itself may not be worth the crowds, Juliet's Balcony and the surrounding courtyard are still iconic landmarks in Verona. Visiting early in the morning or late in the evening will allow you to take in the setting without the crush of tourists. You will still be able to enjoy the romantic ambiance that is Verona's greatest draw.
- **Explore the Museum Inside Casa di Giulietta:** Instead of focusing on the statue, explore the interior of **Casa di Giulietta**, which houses a museum dedicated to the history and legend of Romeo and Juliet. The museum offers intriguing displays of Verona's romantic past in addition to a deeper connection to Shakespeare's story.
- **Visit Juliet's Tomb:** Another lesser-known but significant site is **Juliet's Tomb**, located at the **Monastery of San Francesco al Corso**. It connects to the Romeo and Juliet legend and is far less crowded than Juliet's Balcony. It also offers a quieter, more contemplative experience.

ADDITIONAL TIPS

- **Focus on the Architecture**: The courtyard of Casa di Giulietta is beautiful in its own right, with charming balconies, ivy-covered walls, and an air of romance. Instead of engaging in the custom of rubbing the statues, take some time to enjoy the atmosphere.

- **Write a Letter to Juliet**: Consider engaging in another unusual custom, which is writing a letter to Juliet rather than rubbing the statue. Visitors can leave love letters in the courtyard, and the **Juliet Club** responds to them, keeping the romantic spirit alive in a more meaningful way.

By skipping the modern tourist ritual of rubbing Juliet's statue and exploring other aspects of the Juliet legend, your experience in Verona will be more genuine and pleasurable.

6. DON'T VISIT DURING THE OPERA FESTIVAL WITHOUT PLANNING

Verona is home to the **Arena di Verona**, one of the most famous and well-preserved Roman amphitheaters in the world. Every summer, the city hosts the **Verona Opera Festival**, a world-class event that draws opera lovers from around the globe. While visiting Verona during this time without prior planning can result in disappointment and logistical headaches, attending the festival is a fantastic experience.

WHY SHOULD YOU AVOID IT?

The Verona Opera Festival is one of the city's most popular events and the demand for tickets, accommodations, and restaurants skyrockets during the summer months. If you try to attend a performance or even just visit the city without booking in advance, you may find yourself struggling to secure tickets or paying inflated prices for hotels and dining. Plans made at the last minute may leave you disappointed or overcharged, as many of the best opera performances sell out months in advance.

Even if you're not going to the opera, the city gets busier during the festival season due to the influx of tourists. Popular tourist spots like the Arena, Piazza Bra, and Piazza delle Erbe can be swamped with visitors, leading to long lines and a less enjoyable experience overall.

WHAT TO DO INSTEAD?

- **Plan Ahead:** It's imperative to make travel arrangements well in advance if you wish to attend the Verona Opera Festival. Book your tickets as soon as they go on sale—usually several months before the event. Similarly, secure accommodations early to avoid high prices or limited availability. This will ensure a smooth and enjoyable visit, allowing you to fully immerse yourself in the magic of the opera under the stars.
- **Consider Off-Season Visits:** If seeing the opera isn't your top priority, think about going to Verona during the off-peak summer months. The city is just as beautiful and historic in the spring or fall, with fewer tourists and more affordable accommodations. You'll have more space to explore the city's attractions, and the atmosphere will be more relaxed.
- **Attend a Different Event or Concert:** Check the schedule for concerts and other events if you want to see live performances in the Arena, even if you can't make it to the opera festival. The Arena hosts various musical performances throughout the year, many of which are just as spectacular but less crowded than the summer opera shows.

ADDITIONAL TIPS

- **Dress Code:** If you decide to go to the opera, note that there is a casual dress code in the upper tiers, but for more exclusive seating, formal attire is expected.
- **Arrive Early:** Whether you're just stopping by the Arena or going to an opera, arrive early to avoid the crowds and enjoy the atmosphere of this ancient venue before the show begins.

If you plan ahead or choose to visit Verona outside of the busy Opera Festival season, you'll have a more enjoyable and stress-free experience in this beautiful city.

7. AVOID OVERPRICED SOUVENIRS NEAR MAJOR ATTRACTIONS

Verona is a city full of history, romance, and beautiful sights, but like many tourist hotspots, it's easy to get caught up in buying overpriced souvenirs near popular attractions like **Juliet's Balcony**, **Piazza delle Erbe**, and the **Arena di Verona**. There are a lot of vendors in these places offering trinkets for sale, but a lot of them are mass-produced goods with exorbitant prices.

WHY SHOULD YOU AVOID IT?

Around Verona's most well-known landmarks, souvenir shops and street vendors frequently sell mass-produced, generic goods that lack authenticity. Common souvenirs like keychains, postcards, T-shirts, and figurines may have a Verona-themed design, but they're often cheaply made and identical to those found in tourist areas across Italy. Additionally, prices in these shops are much higher than what you'd pay elsewhere in the city or in local markets.

Buying these items not only costs you more money but also leaves you with a souvenir that doesn't truly capture the unique essence of Verona. These tourist stores aren't the greatest choice if you're searching for something more significant and representative of your journey.

WHAT TO DO INSTEAD?

- **Visit Local Artisan Shops:** Explore the smaller artisan stores strewn throughout Verona's side streets and neighborhoods for genuine, locally made souvenirs. These stores offer unique, handmade goods, such as **ceramics**, **jewelry**, and **hand-painted pottery**, that reflect the city's rich cultural heritage. You will take with you a unique memento created by regional artisans.
- **Explore Verona's Markets:** Another great alternative is to visit Verona's local markets, like the one at **Piazza delle Erbe** (which transforms into a market on certain days). Here, you can find regional products like **Amarone wine**, **Bardolino olive oil**, or **local cheeses**. These are great

keepsakes and presents that accurately capture the regional specialties and handicrafts.
- **Look for Locally Made Products**: Make sure the item is made locally by reading the labels whenever you go shopping for souvenirs. Items labeled **Made in Italy**, or better yet, **Made in Verona**, are often of higher quality and more reflective of the city's traditions than mass-produced items.

ADDITIONAL TIPS

- **Avoid Last-Minute Purchases**: Take your time to explore Verona and its shops before deciding on a souvenir. Rushing into a purchase close to a popular destination frequently results in overpaying for an unexceptionally ordinary item.
- **Support Small Businesses**: By making purchases at nearby artisan stores, you're not only buying a better-quality item but also supporting small businesses that contribute to the local economy.

By avoiding the overpriced, mass-produced souvenirs near Verona's major attractions and seeking out authentic, locally-made items, you'll bring home a memento that perfectly captures Verona's elegance and artistry.

8. DON'T SPEND TOO MUCH TIME IN VERONA WITHOUT EXPLORING NEARBY

In addition to being a lovely city with romantic streets, historical sites, and a vibrant culture, Verona is also perfectly situated close to some of the most breathtaking locations in Northern Italy. Spending all your time in Verona, while tempting, means missing out on nearby gems that are well worth a day trip.

WHY SHOULD YOU AVOID IT?

Even though Verona is a small city with a lot of history and beauty, you can see the majority of its top attractions in a few days. If you limit yourself to just Verona, you might miss out on the opportunity to see other breathtaking places in the surrounding region. Additionally, while Verona is undoubtedly charming, many of the nearby destinations offer entirely different landscapes and experiences that can enrich your trip.

- By not venturing out, you might miss the chance to explore the stunning shores of **Lake Garda**, the cultural richness of **Mantua**, or even the grandeur of **Venice**, which can be reached with a quick train ride.

WHAT TO DO INSTEAD?

- **Take a Day Trip to Lake Garda:** Just a 30-minute train ride from Verona, **Lake Garda** is Italy's largest lake, offering stunning views, charming lakeside villages, and opportunities for boat rides or swimming. Towns like **Sirmione** and **Desenzano del Garda** are easily accessible and provide a refreshing change of pace from city life.
- **Explore Mantua:** The historic city of **Mantua** (Mantova) is another excellent day trip option, located about an hour from Verona by train. It's known for its Renaissance architecture, art, and UNESCO World Heritage Sites. **Palazzo Ducale** and **Palazzo Te** are must-see attractions, and the laid-back vibe of the city complements Verona's tourist attractions well.
- **Visit Venice for a Day:** Venice is a convenient and well-known day trip destination from Verona, just an hour's ride away by train. Whether you've never been or want to revisit its canals and bridges, Venice offers a unique experience that complements your time in Verona.
- **Discover Valpolicella Wine Country:** Just outside of Verona, the **Valpolicella** wine region is a great place to explore if you're a wine enthusiast. Take a wine-tasting tour and learn about **Amarone** wine production while enjoying the beautiful countryside.

ADDITIONAL TIPS

- **Use Trains for Easy Travel:** Northern Italy has an efficient train system, making it easy and affordable to travel between cities and regions. Take a few day trips to discover the region around Verona without having to deal with car rentals.

- **Check Local Events**: Sometimes nearby towns host special festivals or markets, which can offer a unique cultural experience not found in Verona. See if any of these events coincide with your visit by looking at the schedules.

By incorporating a few day trips into your Verona itinerary, you'll enhance your trip with new landscapes, cultural experiences, and exciting adventures outside the city limits.

9. AVOID BUYING SKIP-THE-LINE TICKETS FROM UNOFFICIAL VENDORS

When visiting popular attractions in Verona, such as the **Arena di Verona** or **Juliet's Balcony**, you may encounter street vendors or online platforms offering "skip-the-line" tickets. Although it may be alluring to skip the lengthy lines, purchasing tickets from unofficial sources may result in issues like overspending or even falling for fraud.

WHY SHOULD YOU AVOID IT?

Unofficial vendors often charge significantly higher prices for skip-the-line tickets, sometimes doubling or tripling the actual cost. In addition, tickets purchased from unauthorized sources may not be valid, leaving you unable to enter the attraction and having to buy another ticket at the official booth. These con artists prey on tourists who are ignorant of the true cost of the tickets, and they are especially prevalent in the vicinity of popular tourist destinations.

Moreover, in some cases, these vendors don't provide any real advantage—especially in less crowded seasons when lines aren't as long as advertised. Paying extra for the promise of skipping the line might not be necessary, particularly if you visit during off-peak hours.

WHAT TO DO INSTEAD?

- **Buy Tickets from Official Websites**: Get your tickets straight from the official websites of the attractions you intend to visit at all times. This ensures you're getting legitimate tickets at the correct price, and many official sites also offer skip-the-line options. For the **Arena di Verona**, for example, tickets can be easily purchased online in advance, giving you peace of mind.

- **Visit Early in the Morning or Late in the Afternoon:** Choose a less busy time of day to visit if you want to avoid standing in line but don't want to pay more for skip-the-line tickets. Arriving early in the morning when the attraction opens or later in the afternoon will often allow you to avoid the busiest hours and experience the site with fewer people.
- **Check for Authorized Ticket Vendors:** Make sure the third party you are booking through is an authorized ticket seller. Skip-the-line services are provided by numerous respectable travel agencies, but it's crucial to confirm their legitimacy. Websites like **GetYourGuide** or **Viator** can be trusted as they are partnered with the official ticket distributors for many attractions.

ADDITIONAL TIPS

- **Use Mobile Tickets:** Many official websites offer mobile tickets that you can download and scan at the entrance. This can save you time and the hassle of printing physical tickets.
- **Beware of Pressure Sales:** Street vendors who aggressively pressure you into buying tickets are often a red flag. Prior to making a purchase, always take your time to verify the source.

By avoiding unofficial vendors and sticking to authorized sources for skip-the-line tickets, you'll save money and ensure a smooth visit to Verona's top attractions without the risk of scams.

10. DON'T FORGET TO CHECK THE OPENING HOURS OF MUSEUMS AND CHURCHES

Verona is home to many incredible museums, churches, and historic sites, such as the **Verona Cathedral, Basilica di San Zeno,** and the **Castelvecchio Museum**. However, many of these attractions have specific opening hours that can vary greatly, especially on weekends or holidays. Finding out a website is closed when you get there can be annoying and a waste of time.

WHY SHOULD YOU AVOID IT?

Many of Verona's attractions, particularly its churches, have more restricted opening hours than larger cities, which typically have more regular and extended hours. Some sites close for a long lunch break in the afternoon (typically from 12:30 PM to 3:00 PM), while others may be closed entirely on Sundays or certain holidays. If you don't check the opening times ahead of your visit, you may arrive at a site that is unexpectedly closed or find yourself missing key attractions due to poor planning.

Furthermore, the hours of churches and museums vary frequently based on the season. During the off-season, many attractions reduce their hours, and some may even close earlier in the day.

WHAT TO DO INSTEAD?

- **Check Opening Hours in Advance:** Check the official website or the local tourist office for the hours of operation before visiting any museum or church. Websites like **Museo di Castelvecchio** or **Verona's tourism board** will provide up-to-date information about when these sites are open, helping you plan your visit efficiently.
- **Plan Around Afternoon Closures:** It's best to schedule your visits for early in the morning or late in the afternoon after they reopen because many churches and some museums close in the afternoon for a long break. Use the midday closure to enjoy a leisurely lunch or explore outdoor attractions like **Piazza Bra** or the **Giardino Giusti** Gardens, which remain

- **Use Verona's Tourism App:** Verona offers a helpful tourism app that provides information about local attractions, including opening hours, guided tours, and special events. Planning your day with the app can help you avoid missing anything important because of unforeseen closures.

ADDITIONAL TIPS

- **Holiday Closures:** Be aware of local holidays and religious festivals, as churches and museums may close for special services or events.
- **Purchase Combined Tickets:** Some museums and churches offer combined tickets for multiple attractions. If you're visiting several sites in one day, purchasing a combo ticket can save you time and money; however, make sure to verify the specific opening hours for every website.

By checking the opening hours of museums and churches ahead of time, you'll avoid disappointment and make the most of your time exploring Verona's rich cultural heritage.

Verona is a city rich in romance, history, and stunning architecture, but like any well-traveled place, it's simple to fall victim to typical tourist traps. By knowing what to avoid—whether it's overpriced restaurants, overcrowded attractions, or scams—you can focus on what makes Verona truly special. From wandering its charming streets and discovering hidden gems to exploring nearby destinations like Lake Garda and Venice, a well-planned trip ensures that you'll experience the best this city has to offer.

You can avoid the pitfalls and take in Verona's amazing heritage, cuisine, and culture in a more genuine and fulfilling way with careful planning and a few insider tips. By steering clear of tourist-heavy areas, respecting local traditions, and making time for quieter, off-the-beaten-path experiences, you'll leave Verona with unforgettable memories of one of Italy's most enchanting cities.

BOLOGNA

Bologna, known as **La Grassa** (The Fat One) for its rich culinary heritage, is a city that tantalizes the senses. Home to the famous **Bolognese sauce** and traditional handmade **tortellini**, it's a haven for food lovers. Beyond its gastronomic fame, Bologna boasts stunning medieval architecture, Europe's oldest university, and a vibrant street culture. Bologna, with its recognizable **Two Towers** (Le Due Torri) and meandering porticoes crisscrossing the city, is the epitome of modern Italian life combined with history and culture.

But Bologna has its share of tourist traps and potential blunders that can spoil the experience, just like any other popular destination. Whether it's dealing with crowds at key sites, navigating complex transportation options, or avoiding overpriced eateries, knowing what to skip can save time and money while ensuring a more authentic visit.

This guide will help you discover the best of Bologna while sidestepping common tourist mistakes, allowing you to truly enjoy the city's rich history, incredible food, and lively local atmosphere.

1. AVOID EATING NEAR PIAZZA MAGGIORE

Piazza Maggiore is the beating heart of Bologna, surrounded by stunning medieval architecture, including **Basilica di San Petronio** and **Palazzo dei Banchi**. It's a must-visit spot for sightseeing, but when it comes to dining, the restaurants and cafés nearby can often leave much to be desired. Many of the restaurants in and around the square serve food that isn't authentically Bolognese and are overpriced to appeal mainly to tourists.

WHY SHOULD YOU AVOID IT?

While the idea of dining with a view of Piazza Maggiore sounds appealing, the restaurants in this area tend to be overpriced. You'll often find dishes that are more expensive than elsewhere in the city, and the food quality doesn't always match the high price tag. Instead of the rich, regional flavors that Bologna is known for, you might find more generic Italian dishes on these menus, which are usually created to appeal to tourists from other countries.

Furthermore, because these tourist-focused eateries prioritize filling orders over providing a memorable dining experience, service at these establishments is occasionally hurried. If you're hoping to enjoy traditional dishes like **tagliatelle al ragù** (Bolognese sauce) or **tortellini in brodo** in an authentic setting, you'll likely be disappointed.

WHAT TO DO INSTEAD?

- **Explore Neighborhood Trattorias:** Go a little further from Piazza Maggiore into the local neighborhoods and side streets of Bologna for a more genuine meal. Trattorias and osterias away from the main square offer traditional Bolognese dishes at more reasonable prices and with better quality. Areas like **Via del Pratello** and **Via delle Pescherie Vecchie** are great places to find small, family-run restaurants that serve delicious, local cuisine.
- **Try Osterias for Local Dishes:** Bologna is famous for its osterias—traditional, informal eateries that focus on local food. Places like **Osteria dell'Orsa** or **Trattoria da Gianni** offer an authentic taste of Bologna's rich culinary traditions. These places put tradition, quality, and flavor before visitor appeal.
- **Ask Locals for Recommendations:** Bolognese locals take pride in their food, and they're often happy to share recommendations for the best places to eat. If you ask around, you'll probably find some undiscovered restaurants serving genuinely authentic food.

ADDITIONAL TIPS

- **Avoid "Tourist Menus"**: Restaurants that offer menus in multiple languages and promote special "tourist menus" are often more focused on quantity than quality.
- **Look for Seasonal Dishes**: Authentic Bolognese restaurants use seasonal ingredients, so look for dishes featuring truffles, mushrooms, or fresh vegetables based on the season.

By avoiding the overpriced restaurants near Piazza Maggiore and exploring Bologna's smaller, family-run trattorias, you'll enjoy a more authentic and flavorful experience in one of Italy's best food cities.

2. DON'T CLIMB BOTH TOWERS

Bologna's **Two Towers—Torre degli Asinelli** and **Torre Garisenda**—are iconic symbols of the city and a must-see for visitors. While it's tempting to want to climb both towers for the full experience, only one of them, **Torre degli Asinelli**, is open to the public, and that climb alone is more than enough to get a stunning view of the city. It is superfluous and could be a repetitive and tiring experience to climb both towers.

WHY SHOULD YOU AVOID IT?

First, because of its considerable tilt, Torre Garisenda, the smaller of the two towers, is off-limits to the public. While both towers are famous landmarks in Bologna, Torre Garisenda is not accessible for climbing. So, attempting to visit both may lead to disappointment.

Furthermore, ascending Torre degli Asinelli by yourself is a fulfilling but taxing experience, requiring 498 steep wooden steps to reach the summit. The views from Torre degli Asinelli are panoramic and offer the best vantage point of Bologna's red rooftops and surrounding countryside. Once you've climbed Asinelli, there's no need to search for a similar experience elsewhere in the city.

WHAT TO DO INSTEAD?

- **Climb Torre degli Asinelli Only:** Torre degli Asinelli is more than sufficient to provide you with the complete tower experience in Bologna, provided you are willing to climb it. The tower is 97 meters tall, and the climb is a challenging but rewarding way to see the city from above. Be sure to book your ticket in advance, as the number of visitors allowed is limited.
- **Visit Torre Garisenda from the Ground:** Torre Garisenda, while closed for climbing, can still be admired from below. It's much shorter and leans significantly due to ground settling over the centuries, making it an interesting contrast to the taller Torre degli Asinelli. You can get a sense of the medieval history and architecture of Bologna by visiting both towers.
- **Explore Other Scenic Spots:** If you're looking for other panoramic views without the climb, consider visiting **San Michele in Bosco** or the **Sanctuary of the Madonna di San Luca**. Both provide stunning views of Bologna's surroundings with a lot less work.

ADDITIONAL TIPS

- **Plan Your Climb for a Clear Day:** If you want to make the most of the views from Torre degli Asinelli, check the weather before climbing. Clear, sunny days are ideal for taking in the panorama.
- **Be Prepared for the Climb:** The 498 steps are steep and narrow, so wear comfortable shoes and take your time. The view at the top is well worth the effort.

By limiting your climb to Torre degli Asinelli and appreciating the rest of Bologna's beauty from ground level or alternative viewpoints, you'll make the most of your time without overexerting yourself.

3. AVOID VISITING DURING THE AUGUST HOLIDAY

Bologna is a year-round destination known for its rich history, culinary excellence, and vibrant student culture. However, if you visit during the month of August, particularly around **Ferragosto** (August 15), you may find the city quieter than expected and many businesses closed. This is because August is when a lot of Italians take their summer vacations, which means that there are less open eateries, stores, and tourist attractions in places like Bologna.

WHY SHOULD YOU AVOID IT?

August is traditionally the month when Italians, including many Bolognese locals, head to the coast or countryside to escape the heat. As a result, many restaurants, especially the smaller family-run trattorias, close for weeks, leaving fewer options for dining and exploring the authentic local food scene. It may be difficult to enjoy Bologna's renowned gastronomy and artisanal culture during this period as stores and markets may close.

The city can also have an unusually quiet feel to it, with fewer locals and a more touristy vibe. The hot summer weather in Bologna can also be uncomfortable for sightseeing, especially when many attractions are operating on limited schedules or are closed entirely.

WHAT TO DO INSTEAD?

- **Visit in the Spring or Fall:** Bologna is at its best in the spring (April to June) or fall (September to November). During these seasons, the weather is mild, and the city is bustling with locals and students. All of the well-known eateries, marketplaces, and cultural events in the city will be open to you without the August closures.
- **Check Business Hours in Advance:** If August is your only option for visiting, be sure to check ahead for restaurant closures and plan accordingly. Some popular spots may remain open, but it's essential to have backup options. The locations that are still open during this time can be found by using internet resources or by speaking with locals.

- **Escape to Nearby Destinations:** If you do visit Bologna in August and find many places closed, consider taking day trips to nearby destinations like **Florence, Ravenna,** or **Lake Garda**. You can still find a lot of free attractions and places to eat in these areas, which will give you a more comprehensive understanding of the area.

ADDITIONAL TIPS

- **Expect Higher Prices in Open Restaurants:** Some restaurants that remain open during August may charge higher prices due to the reduced competition. Be prepared for slightly inflated costs.
- **Visit Museums and Churches:** Many of Bologna's museums and churches remain open in August, even if restaurants and shops are closed. Take this opportunity to visit the city's historical sites.

By avoiding a visit to Bologna during the August holiday period, or by planning carefully if you must visit then, you'll ensure a richer and more fulfilling experience of the city.

4. DON'T RELY ON PUBLIC TRANSPORTATION FOR SHORT DISTANCES

Bologna is a city best explored on foot, especially in its historic center, where the streets are filled with architectural marvels, vibrant piazzas, and its famous **porticoes**. Public transportation can be helpful for longer trips, but depending solely on it for short trips within the city can be ineffective and deprive you of the experience of exploring this lovely city on foot.

WHY SHOULD YOU AVOID IT?

- The historic center of Bologna is small and very walkable. The city's unique portico-covered sidewalks stretch for miles, offering shade from the sun and shelter from rain, making walking both practical and enjoyable year-round. Many of the city's key attractions, such as **Piazza Maggiore**, the **Two Towers**, and **Archiginnasio Library**, are all located within close proximity, and walking allows you to appreciate the city's rich history and lively atmosphere up close.

Public transportation, such as buses, is not always the most efficient way to get around within the city center. Traffic congestion can slow down buses, and figuring out the right routes may be time-consuming for short trips. Furthermore, it's possible that the wait times for taxis or buses will exceed the amount of time it takes to walk between locations.

WHAT TO DO INSTEAD?

- **Walk the Historic Center:** Strolling around Bologna's treasures is the best way to experience them. The city's porticoes, which span nearly 40 kilometers, provide a pleasant and shaded walking experience. Strolling through Bologna allows you to easily stop and enjoy the city's hidden gems, including small cafés, shops, and historical landmarks that you might otherwise miss if you rely on buses or taxis.
- **Use Public Transportation for Longer Trips:** If you plan to visit locations outside of the city center, such as **FICO Eataly World** or **Santuario di San Luca**, public transportation like buses or the city's bike-sharing services can be useful. Buses are a cost-effective and efficient mode of transportation for longer distances, but walking is much more satisfying for shorter ones.
- **Rent a Bike:** Since Bologna is bike-friendly, renting a bike is an excellent way to get around without using the public transportation system. Several bike rental stations are scattered around the city, allowing you to cover more ground while still enjoying the fresh air and direct access to Bologna's streets.

ADDITIONAL TIPS

- **Wear Comfortable Shoes**: Bologna's cobblestone streets can be uneven, so make sure you wear comfortable walking shoes to fully enjoy your exploration.
- **Take Your Time:** The leisurely pace of walking in Bologna is one of its

many delights. Take the opportunity to explore its side streets, discover its vibrant markets, or enjoy a coffee in one of its many cafés.

By avoiding public transportation for short distances and choosing to walk or bike instead, you'll have a more immersive and enjoyable experience of Bologna's unique atmosphere and architecture.

5. AVOID THE CENTRAL MARKETS AT PEAK HOURS

Bologna's central markets, such as **Mercato di Mezzo** and **Mercato delle Erbe**, are must-visit spots for anyone interested in local food culture. They serve classic Bolognese dishes, cured meats, fresh produce, and regional cheeses. However, visiting these markets during peak hours—particularly lunchtime or early afternoon—can lead to an overcrowded and overwhelming experience.

WHY SHOULD YOU AVOID IT?

During peak hours, especially around lunch, the central markets become packed with locals and tourists alike, making it difficult to move through the stalls or enjoy a leisurely experience. Lines for food stalls and popular eateries can be long, and seating in shared dining areas can be scarce. Although lively, the crowded environment can take away from the delight of tasting regional specialties because you might feel hurried or find it difficult to find a place to sit down and enjoy your food.

Additionally, the markets can become quite noisy during these busy times, which can make it harder to engage with vendors, ask questions, or fully appreciate the quality and variety of products on offer. The best way to have a more intimate and laid-back experience is to avoid the busiest times.

WHAT TO DO INSTEAD?

- **Visit Early in the Morning:** Visit the markets first thing in the morning for the greatest experience. You'll find them less crowded, giving you plenty of space to browse the stalls, interact with vendors, and enjoy the

freshest offerings of the day. The quieter atmosphere also allows you to take your time exploring the various food items without the pressure of crowds.
- **Go in the Late Afternoon:** If you can't visit the markets in the mornings, you might want to consider going in the late afternoon. The lunch rush will have subsided, and you'll still have access to a wide selection of foods, though some stalls may start to wind down toward closing time. The late afternoon is also a great time to enjoy an aperitivo and sample smaller dishes.
- **Enjoy a Sit-Down Meal Nearby:** If you want to experience Bolognese cuisine during peak hours, consider visiting a nearby restaurant or trattoria instead of trying to eat inside the crowded market. Near the markets are lots of excellent restaurants that serve traditional dishes in a more laid-back atmosphere.

ADDITIONAL TIPS

- Explore Beyond
- **d the Main Halls:** Some of the smaller, less crowded stalls can be found away from the main hall of the market. These sellers offer a more individualized shopping experience in addition to selling distinctive, handcrafted goods.
- **Ask for Tasting Samples:** When the markets aren't too busy, vendors are often happy to offer samples of their products, such as cheeses or meats, allowing you to try them before you buy.

By avoiding the central markets during peak hours and opting for quieter times, you'll have a more enjoyable and less stressful experience while exploring Bologna's vibrant food culture.

6. SKIP TOURIST SOUVENIR SHOPS NEAR THE TWO TOWERS

Bologna's **Two Towers—Torre degli Asinelli** and **Torre Garisenda**—are some of the city's most famous landmarks, and the area around them is often filled with tourists. Although it could be alluring to purchase a souvenir from one of the surrounding shops, these establishments typically sell inflated, mass-produced goods that don't accurately capture the genuine artistry or culture of Bologna.

WHY SHOULD YOU AVOID IT?

The souvenir shops around the Two Towers and other major tourist spots tend to focus on selling generic items like magnets, postcards, T-shirts, and figurines. Many of these products are not locally made and can be found in other tourist-heavy cities across Italy. Because of the heavy foot traffic in these areas, prices are frequently inflated, and the quality of the items is typically subpar.

If you're looking for a meaningful and authentic keepsake from your trip to Bologna, these tourist shops will likely leave you disappointed. Purchasing something ostentatious and mass-produced takes away from the special experience of being in this energetic, old city.

WHAT TO DO INSTEAD?

- **Seek Out Local Artisan Shops:** Numerous skilled craftspeople who produce jewelry, ceramics, leather goods, and traditional crafts can be found in Bologna. Explore smaller shops in neighborhoods like **Via Santo Stefano** or **Via dell'Indipendenza**, where you can find locally made products that reflect Bologna's cultural heritage. These items make for much more meaningful and unique souvenirs.
- **Visit Local Food Markets:** Bologna is regarded as the culinary capital of Italy, and food-related mementos make some of the greatest gifts to bring home. At local markets like **Mercato delle Erbe** or specialty shops like

Tamburini, you can purchase authentic Bolognese products such as **Parmigiano-Reggiano, Modena balsamic vinegar**, or artisanal pasta. These edible souvenirs are a great way to bring a taste of Bologna back home.

- **Look for Locally Produced Items:** When purchasing mementos, make sure the item is manufactured in Bologna, Italy, by carefully reading the labels. Look for products that reflect the region's craftsmanship, whether it's hand-painted ceramics or locally-produced olive oil. Supporting local artisans not only gives you a high-quality souvenir but also helps preserve traditional craftsmanship.

ADDITIONAL TIPS

- **Explore Artisanal Markets:** Bologna hosts several markets where local artists sell their handmade goods. Keep an eye out for craft fairs or weekend markets that showcase local talent.
- **Ask Locals for Recommendations:** If you're unsure where to find authentic souvenirs, ask locals for recommendations. They can frequently direct you to markets or hidden gem stores that offer premium, regionally produced goods.

By skipping the touristy souvenir shops near the Two Towers and seeking out authentic, locally crafted goods, you'll bring home a meaningful and memorable piece of Bologna.

7. DON'T RUSH THROUGH BOLOGNA IN A DAY

Bologna is a city worth spending more time in, as evidenced by its impressive medieval architecture, world-class cuisine, and rich history. Many travelers make the mistake of treating Bologna as a brief stopover, spending just one day here before moving on to other popular destinations like Florence or Venice. However, rushing through Bologna means missing out on its unique charm and hidden gems.

WHY SHOULD YOU AVOID IT?

- While it's possible to see a few key attractions, such as **Piazza Maggiore** and the **Two Towers**, in a single day, you won't be able to fully appreciate what Bologna has to offer if you rush through. The real charm of the city is found in the little things, like its unmatched culinary scene, winding porticoes, local markets, and secret courtyards. Hurrying through these experiences will leave you with only a surface-level understanding of what makes Bologna so special.
- Bologna is also home to countless historic sites, museums, and beautiful churches that require time to explore properly. Sites like **Archiginnasio of Bologna, Santo Stefano complex**, and the many art galleries deserve more than just a cursory glance. Furthermore, if you're in a rush, you'll miss the chance to linger over a leisurely lunch at a trattoria or sip an aperitivo at a café. The laid-back pace of Italian life is best enjoyed slowly.

WHAT TO DO INSTEAD?

- **Stay for at Least Two Days:** To truly experience Bologna, plan to stay for at least two days. This will give you enough time to visit its most famous landmarks while also allowing for leisurely walks through its streets, spontaneous discoveries, and, of course, ample time to enjoy its incredible food scene. Spend some time exploring the vibrant local markets and enjoying a leisurely meal at one of the city's well-known osterias.
- **Explore Beyond the Main Attractions:** While **Piazza Maggiore** and the **Two Towers** are must-sees, don't limit yourself to the main tourist spots. Visit the **University District**, stroll under the porticoes of **Via Zamboni**, and explore the lesser-known **Santo Stefano complex**. These locations provide a more genuine look into the past and culture of Bologna.
- **Take a Food Tour:** Bologna is Italy's gastronomic capital, so no visit is complete without indulging in its cuisine. Book a food tour or cooking class to learn about traditional dishes like **tortellini** and **tagliatelle al ragù**. This immersive experience will leave you with a deeper appreciation for Bolognese culture.

ADDITIONAL TIPS

- **Plan for a Relaxed Pace**: Keep your itinerary from being overly packed. Bologna is best enjoyed slowly, so leave room for spontaneity and time to enjoy the city's cafés and markets.
- **Stay Overnight**: Bologna's nightlife is vibrant, with plenty of bars, jazz clubs, and late-night trattorias. You can see a different side of the city after sundown if you stay the night.

By spending more than just a single day in Bologna and exploring the city at a slower pace, you'll be able to fully immerse yourself in its rich history, culture, and culinary delights.

8. AVOID SKIPPING THE UNIVERSITY DISTRICT

The oldest university in Europe, the **University of Bologna**, was established in 1088 and has played a significant role in the intellectual history of the city. Many visitors focus solely on Bologna's famous landmarks like **Piazza Maggiore** and the **Two Towers**, but skipping the University District means missing out on a vibrant and historically significant part of the city.

WHY SHOULD YOU AVOID IT?

- The University District is a lively area full of historical significance and youthful energy. Walking through its streets gives you a chance to see a different side of Bologna, where academia meets modern-day student life. One of the key sites in this area is the **Archiginnasio of Bologna**, a former university building that houses the **Teatro Anatomico**, an extraordinary 17th-century wooden anatomy theater. This intriguing location is evidence of Bologna's long history in medical and educational research.

Beyond the history, the University District is a great place to experience Bologna's vibrant student culture. The area is packed with affordable cafés, bars, and eateries that cater to students, making it the perfect place to enjoy authentic, budget-friendly meals. In addition, the neighborhood has a diverse array of street art, which gives it a unique and rebellious feel in contrast to the city's more conventional landmarks.

WHAT TO DO INSTEAD?

- **Visit the Archiginnasio and Teatro Anatomico:** Take time to explore the **Archiginnasio**, one of the most important historical buildings in Bologna. Inside, the **Teatro Anatomico** offers a unique glimpse into the city's academic past, particularly its pioneering role in medical studies.
- **Wander Down Via Zamboni:** The University District's main thoroughfare, **Via Zamboni**, is dotted with old buildings, libraries, and hangouts for students. A stroll down this street will immerse you in the area's vibrant student life and give you a chance to discover some of Bologna's hidden gems, such as small bookstores and quirky cafés.
- **Sample Local, Affordable Cuisine:** For inexpensive dining, the University District is among Bologna's greatest options. Try local favorites like **piadina** (a flatbread sandwich) or **tagliatelle al ragù** at small trattorias frequented by students, where you can enjoy high-quality, authentic food without the high prices.

ADDITIONAL TIPS

- **Visit During Term Time:** The University District is especially lively during the academic year when students fill the area's cafés, bars, and streets. You can fully experience the lively energy of the district if you visit during this time.

By exploring Bologna's University District, you'll gain a deeper appreciation for the city's rich academic history and enjoy a more authentic, local experience that many tourists miss.

9. DON'T MISS BOOKING A TABLE AT POPULAR RESTAURANTS

Bologna is known as Italy's culinary capital, and its traditional dishes like **tagliatelle al ragù** (Bolognese sauce) and **tortellini in Brodo** are famous worldwide. However, many of Bologna's best restaurants are small, family-run establishments that fill up quickly, especially during weekends. You might be forced to settle for a less special meal if you don't make a reservation in advance.

WHY SHOULD YOU AVOID IT?

Bologna's food scene is highly regarded, and some of its most beloved restaurants, trattorias, and osterias are small with limited seating. These places are often fully booked, especially on weekends, holidays, or during peak tourist season. If you show up without a reservation, you might have to settle for a less genuine or touristy option due to lengthy waits or no table at all.

- Popular spots like **Osteria dell'Orsa** or **Trattoria di Via Serra** are known for their exceptional food and reasonable prices, but they are also in high demand. If you don't plan ahead and miss these highly recommended restaurants, you might miss out on some of the best traditional dishes Bologna has to offer.

WHAT TO DO INSTEAD?

- **Make Reservations in Advance:** Make reservations in advance for any meal, especially dinner. Many restaurants allow online reservations, or you can simply call ahead. Booking ensures that you won't miss out on some of Bologna's most renowned culinary experiences.
- **Consider Eating Outside Peak Hours:** If you find it hard to book a table during traditional meal times, consider dining a little earlier or later than usual. Lunch between 12:00 and 1:00 PM or dinner after 9:00 PM may give you a better chance of finding a spot in popular restaurants.
- **Explore Lesser-Known Trattorias:** While the most famous spots tend to book up quickly, Bologna is full of hidden gems that may not be as well-known but still offer exceptional food. Consult with the locals or look up more sedate locations that are still serving real Bolognese food; they might not need reservations as far in advance.

ADDITIONAL TIPS

- **Don't Forget to Book for Lunch**: Some of Bologna's best places for lunch, like **Trattoria Anna Maria** or **Ristorante Da Cesari**, can also get crowded. Make sure to reserve ahead, even for lunch.
- **Check for Special Menus or Tasting Nights**: Some restaurants offer special tasting menus or themed dinner nights, which may also require reservations. Making reservations in advance guarantees you won't pass up these exceptional dining opportunities.

By making reservations ahead of time, you'll secure your place at Bologna's top restaurants and enjoy the city's renowned cuisine without the stress of finding a last-minute table.

10. AVOID TAXIS AND OPT FOR BIKING

Bologna is a compact and highly walkable city, making it easy to explore on foot or by bike. While taxis may seem convenient, they can be expensive and unnecessary for getting around the city center. Choosing to ride a bike instead will save you money and give you a more immersive experience of the city's famous porticoes and charming streets.

WHY SHOULD YOU AVOID IT?

Taxis in Bologna, like in many Italian cities, can be pricey, especially for short trips within the city center. The cost of a taxi ride can quickly add up, particularly if you're traveling during peak hours or on weekends when fares tend to be higher. Furthermore, getting around Bologna by car or taxi can be inefficient due to the city's small streets and pedestrian zones, as you may encounter traffic jams or have to walk portions of the route.

Bologna is relatively small, and its historic center is best explored by foot or bike. Many areas are restricted to pedestrian traffic or are difficult for taxis to access, meaning you'll likely end up walking to your destination anyway. Cycling lets you take advantage of the lively atmosphere of the city and is a quicker, more flexible, and environmentally friendly mode of transportation.

WHAT TO DO INSTEAD?

- **Rent a Bike:** Bologna is a bike-friendly city with plenty of rental options available. You can rent bikes by the hour or day from stations around the city or from dedicated bike shops. An enjoyable and active way to see Bologna at your own pace is to ride through its streets and under its porticoes.
- **Use the Public Bike-Sharing System:** Bologna has a public bike-sharing program called **Mobike**, which is easy to use and perfect for short trips around the city. Bikes are a handy and reasonably priced way to get around the city, as you can pick them up and drop them off at different locations.
- **Walk Through the City Center:** Bologna's historic center is highly walkable, and many of its most famous sites, like **Piazza Maggiore**, **Via Zamboni**, and the **Two Towers**, are within easy walking distance of each other. You can discover tucked-away spots, go to regional markets, and make stops at cafés while strolling.

ADDITIONAL TIPS

- **Stay Safe While Biking**: Bologna's streets can be busy, so always be cautious when biking, especially in traffic. When available, stay in bike lanes and pay attention to pedestrian areas.
- **Combine Biking and Walking**: Use a bike for longer distances or to quickly get around, but take time to walk through areas where cycling isn't practical, such as narrow streets and piazzas.

By choosing to bike or walk instead of taking taxis, you'll save money, reduce your environmental footprint, and experience Bologna's streets more intimately, making your visit more enjoyable and interactive.

Bologna is a city that invites you to slow down, savor its culinary delights, and immerse yourself in its rich history and vibrant atmosphere. By avoiding common tourist pitfalls—like skipping the University District, rushing through in a day, or missing out on booking popular restaurants—you can experience Bologna in its most authentic form. Bologna is a rewarding place for those who take the time to carefully explore, whether it's by bike through its charming streets, strolling beneath the city's famous porticoes, or having a leisurely meal in a neighborhood trattoria.

With a little planning and awareness of what to avoid, you'll be able to discover the true spirit of this Italian gem, from its hidden artisan shops to its vibrant student life. Allow Bologna's rich history, vibrant culture, and mouthwatering food to lead you on a journey that will never be forgotten.

PISA

Pisa, famous worldwide for its iconic **Leaning Tower**, is a charming city in the Tuscany region with much more to offer than its most photographed landmark. Millions of tourists visit **Piazza dei Miracoli** every year, but there are other attractions worth seeing as well, like the city's rich history, energetic student culture, and lesser-known sights.

That said, like many popular tourist destinations, Pisa comes with its share of potential challenges. From overcrowded sites and overpriced restaurants to missed opportunities for more authentic experiences, it's easy to fall into common tourist traps if you're not careful. You can enjoy your visit much more and get a better sense of Pisa's true nature if you know what to avoid.

This guide highlights 10 key things to avoid while visiting Pisa, ensuring that your time in the city is both rewarding and memorable. These pointers will help you avoid needless stress while exploring Pisa's treasures, whether you're there for a few hours or a full day.

1. AVOID VISITING THE LEANING TOWER AT PEAK TIMES

The **Leaning Tower of Pisa** is undoubtedly the city's most famous landmark, attracting millions of visitors each year. While seeing this architectural marvel in person is a must, visiting during peak hours can quickly turn into a frustrating experience. Long wait times, crowded areas, and few opportunities for pictures can ruin your trip.

WHY SHOULD YOU AVOID IT?

- The Leaning Tower is busiest between late morning and mid-afternoon, when large tour groups, day-trippers, and tourists flood the area. This often results in long queues to enter the tower and overcrowding at **Piazza dei Miracoli**, the site of the tower and other famous buildings like the **Cathedral** and **Baptistery**. Navigating the crowds can make it difficult to fully appreciate the beauty and history of the site. Furthermore, it becomes almost impossible to take a clear picture of the tower without having other people in the background.

Additionally, visiting during these hours can lead to long wait times for both climbing the tower and visiting nearby attractions, leaving you feeling rushed and overwhelmed.

WHAT TO DO INSTEAD?

- **Visit Early in the Morning or Late in the Afternoon:** Plan to visit the Leaning Tower early in the morning, right when it opens, or later in the afternoon, closer to closing time, to avoid the crowds. These times are typically quieter, allowing you to enjoy the experience without fighting through large crowds. You'll also have more space to take photos and appreciate the surroundings.
- **Pre-Book Your Tickets:** Purchase your Leaning Tower tickets online in advance to avoid the lineup and save time. This will allow you to choose a specific time slot, ensuring that you can plan your visit around less busy hours and avoid waiting in long queues.
- **Explore Other Attractions During Peak Hours:** If you find yourself in Pisa during peak times, consider visiting less crowded attractions first, such as **Piazza dei Cavalieri**, **Camposanto Monumentale**, or strolling along the **Arno River**. Later in the day, after the crowds have subsided, you can visit the Leaning Tower again.

ADDITIONAL TIPS

- **Check for Special Events:** Pisa hosts various events and festivals throughout the year that can increase foot traffic around the Leaning Tower. To steer clear of especially busy days, make sure to check the city's

event calendar.
- **Visit During Shoulder Seasons**: If possible, plan your trip during the shoulder seasons (spring or fall) when the weather is pleasant, and there are fewer tourists.

By visiting the Leaning Tower at off-peak times and pre-booking your tickets, you'll enjoy a more peaceful and rewarding experience, free from the stress of large crowds and long waits.

2. SKIP THE OVERPRICED SOUVENIR STANDS NEAR THE TOWER

The area surrounding the **Leaning Tower of Pisa** is packed with souvenir vendors selling everything from T-shirts and magnets to miniature replicas of the tower itself. Although the items sold at these stalls may appear convenient, they are often mass-produced, expensive, and of inferior quality when compared to other locations in the city.

WHY SHOULD YOU AVOID IT?

Souvenir stands near the Leaning Tower cater primarily to tourists, and prices are significantly marked up because of the prime location. Most of the items sold are generic and can be found in other popular tourist destinations across Italy, meaning they lack the unique touch you might want in a keepsake from Pisa. Furthermore, a lot of these items are poorly made and have short shelf lives, which reduces their value as sentimental mementos.

By purchasing from these vendors, you're likely to overpay for a low-quality item that doesn't reflect the true craftsmanship of Tuscany or Pisa.

WHAT TO DO INSTEAD?

- **Explore Local Artisan Shops:** For unique, high-quality souvenirs, venture away from the tourist-heavy areas near Piazza dei Miracoli. Explore the quieter streets of Pisa, where you'll find local artisan shops selling handcrafted goods like **ceramics, leather products**, and **jewelry**. These

products are more genuine and meaningful keepsakes in addition to helping local artists.
- **Visit Pisa's Markets:** Consider visiting local markets like **Pisa's Saturday market** at **Piazza Vittorio Emanuele II**, where you can find a range of interesting goods, from clothing to local produce. For food-related souvenirs, visit traditional delicatessens and shops where you can purchase Tuscan products like **olive oil, wine,** or **pecorino cheese**—all of which make excellent gifts.
- **Buy from Museums:** Many museums in Pisa, such as the **Museo dell'Opera del Duomo,** have gift shops that offer high-quality souvenirs related to the city's art and history. Rather than simply purchasing another mass-produced trinket, these stores offer the chance to take home objects that represent the cultural significance of Pisa.

ADDITIONAL TIPS

- **Look for Authentic "Made in Italy" Labels**: When purchasing souvenirs, make sure they're actually made in Italy. Avoid buying items that are marked with "Made in China" or "Made in PRC," as these are mass-produced for the tourist market.
- **Negotiate Prices if Appropriate**: At certain stalls, especially in markets, there's some room for negotiation. Be polite, and you may be able to get a better deal on more unique items.

By skipping the overpriced souvenir stands near the Leaning Tower and seeking out authentic, locally made products, you'll bring home meaningful mementos that reflect the true spirit of Pisa.

3. DON'T EAT AT RESTAURANTS NEAR PIAZZA DEI MIRACOLI

Piazza dei Miracoli, home to the Leaning Tower of Pisa and other beautiful landmarks, is a major tourist hub. While it's tempting to grab a meal at one of the restaurants nearby, many of these establishments cater specifically to tourists and offer overpriced food of average quality. When you eat here, you frequently wind up paying too much for a subpar meal.

WHY SHOULD YOU AVOID IT?

- The restaurants around **Piazza dei Miracoli** typically charge inflated prices due to their prime location. Although it's handy to be close to Pisa's main attractions, the food is frequently not representative of the genuine Tuscan cuisine for which the area is renowned. Menus tend to feature generic Italian dishes that lack the freshness and flavor you'd expect from traditional local eateries. Additionally, the service in tourist-heavy areas can be rushed, with staff focused on serving a high turnover of visitors rather than providing a memorable dining experience.

Eating here means you'll likely overpay for a meal that falls short of the culinary richness you could experience elsewhere in Pisa.

WHAT TO DO INSTEAD?

- **Venture into Local Neighborhoods:** For an authentic dining experience, head to areas beyond the tourist zone, such as **Borgo Stretto** or the streets around **Piazza delle Vettovaglie**. There are many trattorias and osterias in these neighborhoods that offer excellent Tuscan cuisine at more affordable prices. You'll find traditional dishes like **pappardelle al cinghiale** (wild boar pasta) or **ribollita** (Tuscan bread soup) made with fresh, local ingredients.
- **Look for Small, Family-Run Trattorias:** Family-run trattorias are a hallmark of Italian dining, offering dishes prepared with care and authentic recipes passed down through generations. Places like **Osteria dei Cavalieri** and **Il Campano** provide a true taste of Pisa's culinary heritage in a relaxed, welcoming atmosphere.
- **Ask Locals for Recommendations:** Locals are your best resource when it comes to finding the best food. Don't hesitate to ask shopkeepers, taxi drivers, or your hotel staff for their favorite dining spots. They will probably point you in the direction of hidden gems that offer genuine

Tuscan food without the tourist inflated prices.

ADDITIONAL TIPS

- **Check the Menu for Local Specialties**: Authentic Tuscan restaurants will often have dishes that feature seasonal, regional ingredients. Look for items like **pici pasta, pecorino cheese**, and dishes with truffles or wild game.
- **Avoid Restaurants with Tourist Menus**: If a restaurant displays menus in multiple languages with photos of dishes, it's likely catering to tourists. These places usually provide an expensive and less genuine dining experience.

By avoiding the restaurants near Piazza dei Miracoli and exploring local trattorias in Pisa's quieter neighborhoods, you'll enjoy better food at a more reasonable price while experiencing the true flavors of Tuscany.

4. AVOID STAYING IN PISA FOR A WHOLE DAY

Even though Pisa is a lovely city with the famous Leaning Tower and other historical sites, many tourists make the mistake of spending a whole day exploring it because of its small size. While the **Piazza dei Miracoli** and the **Leaning Tower** are must-sees, Pisa can easily be explored in half a day, allowing you to combine your visit with nearby destinations.

WHY SHOULD YOU AVOID IT?

- Spending a full day in Pisa may leave you with time to spare, as most of the major attractions are concentrated around the **Piazza dei Miracoli**, and once you've seen the Leaning Tower, the **Baptistery**, and the **Cathedral**, there's not much more to fill the rest of the day. After a few hours, you may find yourself searching for activities to do or simply walking around the same areas. Pisa is a well-liked day-trip destination, so during peak hours, the crowds around the tower and major attractions can be unbearable, which makes it even harder to fully enjoy the city.

WHAT TO DO INSTEAD?

- **Combine Pisa with a Trip to Lucca:** A perfect way to optimize your time is by pairing Pisa with a visit to **Lucca**, a beautiful medieval town just 30 minutes away by train. Lucca is known for its well-preserved Renaissance walls, charming streets, and relaxed atmosphere. You can easily spend a few hours exploring its **Piazza dell'Anfiteatro**, climbing **Torre Guinigi**, or enjoying a bike ride along the city walls.
- **Add a Stop in Florence:** If you're heading to Pisa from **Florence**, consider making it a half-day trip. Because Pisa is close to Florence, it's simple to visit the bigger city in the afternoon and continue discovering its gastronomic, artistic, and cultural offerings. Florence offers a much broader array of activities, making it an excellent complement to a brief visit to Pisa.
- **Explore the Tuscan Countryside:** Consider going on a picturesque train or driving through the **Tuscan countryside** after visiting Pisa. Nearby regions like **Chianti** or **Val d'Orcia** offer stunning landscapes, vineyards, and opportunities for wine tastings or leisurely lunches at agriturismos (farm stays).

ADDITIONAL TIPS

- **Visit Pisa Early or Late:** If you only have a few hours in Pisa, consider visiting early in the morning or late in the afternoon. This way, you can avoid the busiest crowds and still have time to explore another nearby city.
- **Use Pisa as a Stopover:** Pisa is well-connected by train, making it a convenient stopover between larger cities like Florence and the coast. To maximize your travel time, plan your itinerary.

By limiting your time in Pisa to a half-day and combining your visit with nearby cities or countryside explorations, you'll make the most of your time in Tuscany without feeling rushed or stuck with nothing to do.

5. SKIP CLIMBING THE TOWER IF YOU'RE CLAUSTROPHOBIC

Climbing the famous **Leaning Tower of Pisa** is a popular activity for many visitors, offering unique views of the city from the top. However, the narrow, spiraling staircases inside the tower can feel quite cramped, especially during peak tourist times. It might not be the greatest experience for you if you have claustrophobia or find small areas uncomfortable.

WHY SHOULD YOU AVOID IT?

The staircase inside the Leaning Tower is narrow and steep, with around 300 steps to the top. The spiral nature of the climb, combined with the tower's iconic tilt, can make the ascent feel disorienting. For those who are claustrophobic, this can quickly become a stressful experience, as there's no easy way to turn back once you've started the climb. The tower may get crowded with other tourists during busy hours, which only heightens the sense of confinement.

Additionally, while the view from the top is impressive, Pisa's flat landscape means you won't get the same dramatic vistas you might expect from other towers in Italy. There won't be much loss if you skip the climb if confined spaces bother you.

WHAT TO DO INSTEAD?

- **Admire the Tower from Below:** The **Leaning Tower of Pisa** is a marvel to look at from ground level. Spend time exploring the **Piazza dei Miracoli**, taking photos from various angles, and appreciating the beauty of the tower's unique architecture without the need to climb it.
- **Climb Other Towers in Tuscany:** If you're still interested in climbing a tower during your trip but want a more open experience, consider climbing the **Torre Guinigi** in **Lucca** or the **Torre del Mangia** in **Siena**. Less cramped spaces can be found in both towers thanks to their roomier staircases and breathtaking views of Tuscany's rolling hills and medieval

buildings.

- **Visit Pisa's Other Monuments:** Instead of climbing the tower, use your time to explore Pisa's other historical sites, such as the **Baptistery**, the **Cathedral**, and the **Camposanto Monumentale**. These beautiful buildings are part of the **Piazza dei Miracoli** complex and offer just as much historical significance as the tower.

ADDITIONAL TIPS

- **Visit the Tower Early or Late:** If you're set on climbing the tower but want to avoid crowds, visit early in the morning or late in the afternoon when it's less busy. The climb may seem less limiting because of the calmer environment.
- **Prepare for the Climb:** If you decide to climb the tower, be prepared for the disorienting effect of the tilt and the narrow staircases. To prevent feeling overburdened, take your time and wear comfortable shoes.

By skipping the climb and enjoying Pisa's landmarks from the ground, or choosing alternative towers in nearby cities, you'll avoid unnecessary stress and still have a fulfilling visit to this iconic city.

6. AVOID VISITING PISA ON CRUISE SHIP DAYS

Pisa, particularly the area around the **Leaning Tower** and **Piazza dei Miracoli**, is a popular stop for cruise ship passengers arriving from nearby ports like **Livorno**. On cruise ship days, the city becomes much more crowded as hundreds or even thousands of tourists flock to Pisa for a quick visit. What should be a calm, enjoyable experience could become crowded and chaotic due to this influx.

WHY SHOULD YOU AVOID IT?

When cruise ships dock, Pisa is flooded with large tour groups, often arriving by bus. These groups tend to visit the same main attractions, such as the Leaning Tower, the Cathedral, and the Baptistery, causing long lines and crowded spaces. The streets around the tourist zone become congested, and finding a quiet spot to enjoy the city's beauty becomes a challenge. In addition, businesses that profit from the increased demand from tourists often raise prices on these busy days for meals, souvenirs, and even parking.

With more people vying for the same attractions, it can be difficult to fully appreciate the architectural beauty and historical significance of Pisa's landmarks. It is also more difficult to take pictures without people in the background due to the busy atmosphere.

WHAT TO DO INSTEAD?

- **Check Cruise Ship Schedules:** Before planning your trip to Pisa, check the cruise ship schedules for the port of Livorno. Websites like **CruiseMapper** or port authority websites provide information on when ships will be docking. You can have a more laid-back visit and stay away from the crowds by avoiding these days.
- **Visit Pisa Early or Late:** If you can't avoid a cruise ship day, consider visiting Pisa early in the morning or late in the afternoon, outside of the peak times when tour groups arrive. A more tranquil visit may be had if you go to Pisa after mid-morning or early in the afternoon when most tours visit the city.
- **Explore Less Crowded Attractions:** Spend less time at the most visited locations, such as the Leaning Tower, on cruise ship days and instead discover some of Pisa's lesser-known treasures. Visit the **Piazza dei Cavalieri**, take a stroll along the **Arno River**, or enjoy the peaceful atmosphere at **Giardino Scotto**, a beautiful public garden.

ADDITIONAL TIPS

- **Plan for Midweek Visits:** Cruise ships often dock on weekends, so visiting Pisa during the middle of the week can help you avoid the busiest days.
- **Book Tickets in Advance:** If you must visit on a cruise ship day, be sure to book tickets for attractions like the Leaning Tower in advance. You can avoid the lengthy lineups brought on by big tour groups by doing this.

By avoiding Pisa on busy cruise ship days or timing your visit to miss the crowds, you'll have a much more enjoyable and relaxed experience in this historic city.

7. DON'T FORGET TO EXPLORE BEYOND THE TOWER

Many visitors come to Pisa with the sole goal of seeing the Leaning Tower, often missing out on the other beautiful and historically significant sites the city has to offer. Even though Pisa is known for its iconic Leaning Tower, there is much more to discover than just this site.

WHY SHOULD YOU AVOID IT?

- If you limit your visit to the **Leaning Tower of Pisa** and **Piazza dei Miracoli**, you're missing out on a wealth of culture, history, and local charm that exists beyond these highly touristic spots. Focusing only on the tower means you might overlook other incredible sites, such as the **Camposanto Monumentale**, a stunning cemetery with medieval frescoes, or the **Piazza dei Cavalieri**, an elegant square that was once the political heart of Pisa.

In addition, Pisa has lovely cathedrals, museums, and serene walks along the river that provide a more genuine look into the city's history. If you rush through just to take a photo of the tower and leave, you're likely to miss out on the deeper experience the city has to offer.

WHAT TO DO INSTEAD?

- **Visit the Camposanto and Other Piazza dei Miracoli Monuments:** Spend time exploring the other monuments within the **Piazza dei Miracoli** complex, such as the **Camposanto**, a monumental cemetery, the **Baptistery**, and the **Cathedral of Pisa**. Compared to the tower itself, these locations have less crowds and rich histories along with stunning architecture.
- **Explore Piazza dei Cavalieri:** Just a short walk from Piazza dei Miracoli is **Piazza dei Cavalieri**, one of Pisa's most beautiful squares, known for its Renaissance architecture. The square was once the center of political life

in Pisa and is now home to the prestigious **Scuola Normale Superiore**.
- **Walk Along the Arno River:** Pisa's center is divided by the **Arno River**, which also flows through Florence. A stroll along its banks will give you a peaceful escape from the busy tourist areas and allow you to admire the beautiful **Palazzo Blu** and other historic buildings that line the river.
- **Visit Giardino Scotto:** For a break from sightseeing, head to **Giardino Scotto**, a tranquil public garden perfect for a relaxing afternoon. It's a great place to relax, especially if you're looking for a quiet getaway or are traveling to Pisa with kids.

ADDITIONAL TIPS

- **Check for Local Events**: Pisa often hosts local events, markets, and festivals that give you a deeper sense of the city's culture. Look up events taking place during your visit on the calendars in the area.
- **Explore Pisa's Churches**: Pisa is home to many other beautiful churches beyond the Cathedral, such as **San Michele in Borgo** and **San Paolo a Ripa d'Arno**, each offering its own slice of the city's religious and architectural history.

By taking the time to explore beyond the Leaning Tower, you'll discover a richer, more authentic side of Pisa that many tourists miss, making your visit more fulfilling and memorable.

8. AVOID THE PICKPOCKETS IN CROWDED AREAS

Like many tourist-heavy cities, Pisa has its share of pickpockets, particularly around the most popular attractions such as the **Leaning Tower, Piazza dei Miracoli**, and other crowded spots. A visit that could be enjoyable could also be ruined by theft if you are careless with your possessions.

WHY SHOULD YOU AVOID IT?

Crowded areas like the Piazza dei Miracoli, where tourists are focused on getting the perfect shot of the Leaning Tower, are prime spots for pickpockets to operate. They frequently profit from the excitement of sightseeing and the diversions brought on by big crowds. Pickpockets work quickly, and before you realize it, your wallet, phone, or other valuable items may be gone.

Furthermore, well-known eateries and cafés close to important sites may serve as hubs for small-time theft. Many tourists are unaware of how easily they can be targeted while in a busy setting, especially when carrying open bags or leaving personal items unattended.

WHAT TO DO INSTEAD?

- **Use Anti-Theft Bags:** Invest in an anti-theft bag; these bags typically feature straps that are resistant to slashes, hidden compartments, and locking zippers. Cross-body bags worn in front of you are also harder for pickpockets to access than backpacks or purses slung over your shoulder.
- **Keep Valuables Secure:** Avoid storing important items like your phone, wallet, or passport in easily accessible pockets, especially in crowded areas. Use interior pockets in your clothing or secure compartments in your bag that aren't visible to others. You should only bring what you need for the day and try to leave valuables like jewelry or large sums of cash in a hotel safe.
- **Stay Aware of Your Surroundings:** Being mindful of your surroundings is one of the best defenses against pickpocketing. Keep an eye on your belongings, especially when taking photos or navigating through busy areas. Be especially wary if someone tries to divert your attention by approaching you or asking for assistance; these are common strategies employed by pickpockets.

ADDITIONAL TIPS

- **Avoid Keeping All Valuables in One Place:** Spread your valuables out across different pockets or bags. In this manner, if a pickpocket is successful in grabbing anything, they won't take it all at once.
- **Use a Money Belt or Hidden Pouch:** For extra security, consider using a money belt or hidden pouch under your clothing to store important items like your passport, credit cards, and cash.

By staying vigilant and securing your belongings, you can avoid becoming a target for pickpockets and enjoy your time in Pisa without unnecessary stress.

9. DON'T EXPECT PISA TO BE LIKE FLORENCE OR ROME

Pisa is often compared to its more famous Tuscan neighbor, **Florence**, or even larger cities like **Rome**, but it offers a distinctly different experience. Visitors who arrive expecting the grandeur of these cities may leave feeling underwhelmed if they don't adjust their expectations beforehand. Compared to larger Italian hubs, Pisa is calmer, smaller, and focused on its distinctive medieval landmarks rather than an abundance of art, museums, and bustling city life.

WHY SHOULD YOU AVOID IT?

- You may be let down if you go to Pisa, thinking it will be as large, vibrant, and culturally diverse as Florence or Rome. Pisa's attractions, such as the **Leaning Tower**, the **Cathedral**, and the **Baptistery**, are concentrated within the **Piazza dei Miracoli**. Once you've explored this iconic area, the rest of Pisa feels much quieter, with fewer grand galleries, museums, or bustling streets. While Pisa's architectural beauty is undeniable, it doesn't offer the overwhelming array of historic sites and vibrant neighborhoods that you might expect from cities like Florence or Rome.

But rather than equating Pisa with Italy's more populous cultural centers, it's vital to recognize Pisa for what it is and to enjoy its quiet, slower-paced atmosphere. Pisa is perfect for those who enjoy wandering medieval streets, admiring architecture, and taking in a more laid-back atmosphere.

WHAT TO DO INSTEAD?

- **Embrace Pisa's Relaxed Pace:** Pisa is a city that can be enjoyed at a slower pace. After visiting the **Leaning Tower** and the **Piazza dei Miracoli**, take time to stroll along the **Arno River** or explore the **Piazza dei Cavalieri**, a beautiful square that was once the political center of Pisa. Savor the tranquility of the city and explore its less visited areas.

- **Focus on Pisa's Historical Significance:** Many visitors who are only interested in the Leaning Tower fail to notice Pisa's past as a strong maritime republic in the Middle Ages. Take time to learn about the city's rich past by visiting the **Museo delle Sinopie** or exploring the city's history beyond its famous landmarks.
- **Plan Pisa as a Short Stay:** It's ideal to spend a half-day or overnight visit to Pisa. Pairing Pisa with nearby destinations like **Lucca** or **Florence** allows you to experience the highlights of Tuscany while not overextending your stay in Pisa.

ADDITIONAL TIPS

- **Enjoy the Student Energy:** Pisa is home to the **University of Pisa**, one of Italy's oldest universities, which gives the city a youthful and vibrant energy. Explore the campus area to get a taste of local student life and discover reasonably priced dining and drinking establishments.
- **Appreciate the Architecture:** Pisa's Romanesque and Gothic architecture, especially in the Piazza dei Miracoli, is stunning and unique. Take your time examining the minute details of these sites, ignoring any urge to contrast them with the opulence of Rome or Florence.

By embracing Pisa for its unique qualities and not expecting it to match larger Italian cities, you'll find charm in its quieter streets, historic landmarks, and more relaxed atmosphere.

10. AVOID PUBLIC RESTROOMS NEAR THE TOWER

Public restrooms near the **Leaning Tower of Pisa** and **Piazza dei Miracoli** can often be crowded, poorly maintained, and not very clean. Many visitors find that using these facilities spoils an otherwise enjoyable trip, especially during the busiest travel seasons when cleanliness standards can deteriorate, and lines can get very long.

WHY SHOULD YOU AVOID IT?

Public restrooms in busy tourist areas like Piazza dei Miracoli are frequently used by the thousands of visitors who flock to see the Leaning Tower each day. As a result, they can become overwhelmed, with limited staff to maintain cleanliness throughout the day. Long queues are common, especially around lunchtime or peak visiting hours, and the facilities are often basic at best. The lack of cleanliness, combined with large crowds, can make the experience unpleasant. To make matters more frustrating, some restrooms may even charge a nominal fee to use them.

Furthermore, a lot of these restrooms are situated in busy areas, so getting to them will require you to navigate through crowded areas. If you're on a tight schedule or looking to avoid unnecessary stress, using these public facilities may end up being more trouble than it's worth.

WHAT TO DO INSTEAD?

- **Use Restrooms at Cafés or Restaurants:** A much better option is to take advantage of the facilities in local cafés or restaurants. When you stop for a coffee, snack, or meal, you can use the restroom in a cleaner, more comfortable environment. In Pisa, there are lots of little restaurants that welcome guests, and stopping for a quick espresso can be an excuse to use their spaces.
- **Plan Ahead:** Use the restrooms at less crowded locations before you arrive at the Piazza dei Miracoli if you know you'll be spending some time there. If you're arriving in Pisa by train, consider using the facilities at the **Pisa Centrale** train station before heading to the main attractions.
- **Visit Museums or Cultural Sites:** Pisa's museums, such as the **Museo dell'Opera del Duomo** or other attractions around the Piazza dei Miracoli, often have restrooms that are cleaner and less crowded than the public ones directly around the Leaning Tower. These have better maintenance and are generally more comfortable.

ADDITIONAL TIPS

- **Bring Sanitary Essentials**: Carry hand sanitizer and tissues in case you do have to use a public restroom, as they may not always be well-stocked.

- **Avoid Peak Times**: If you must use a public restroom near the Leaning Tower, try to avoid peak hours (late morning to early afternoon) when crowds are at their highest.

By avoiding the often-overcrowded and poorly maintained public restrooms near the Leaning Tower and opting for cleaner alternatives, you'll have a more pleasant experience during your visit to Pisa.

Beyond just the Leaning Tower, Pisa has a fascinating past, breathtaking architecture, and a calmer, more laid-back vibe than other Italian cities. However, like any popular destination, it comes with its share of tourist traps and potential challenges. By knowing what to avoid—whether it's visiting during peak times, dining at overpriced tourist restaurants, or sticking only to the main attractions—you can enhance your experience and enjoy Pisa in its true charm.

You can discover Pisa's true nature by venturing beyond the Piazza dei Miracoli, spending some time admiring the city's other historical sites, and adjusting to its slower pace of life. From its riverside walks to hidden local trattorias, Pisa rewards those who take the time to venture beyond the crowds.

By following the tips in this guide, you'll navigate Pisa more thoughtfully, avoid common mistakes, and leave with a deeper appreciation of the city's beauty and cultural significance.

TURIN

- Turin, often overshadowed by Italy's more famous cities like Rome, Florence, or Venice, is a gem waiting to be discovered. Tucked away in the Piedmont region at the base of the Alps, Turin is renowned for its magnificent boulevards, tasteful architecture, and deep historical significance. Once the capital of the Kingdom of Italy, it remains a city steeped in culture, boasting world-class museums, such as the **Museo Egizio** and the **National Museum of Cinema**, as well as architectural landmarks like the **Mole Antonelliana**.
- Beyond its historical attractions, Turin provides tourists with a taste of affluent Italian living. From its renowned **aperitivo** culture to its deep-rooted coffee traditions and its status as the birthplace of the **Slow Food** movement, Turin is a paradise for food and drink enthusiasts. The city is also home to a thriving contemporary art scene, vibrant markets, and beautiful parks that come alive in the spring and fall.

Like any well-known location, there are some common mistakes and tourist traps to be aware of. Whether it's navigating the historic streets, finding authentic places to eat, or understanding the local customs, this guide will help you discover the best of Turin while avoiding unnecessary pitfalls.

1. AVOID VISITING ONLY THE SHROUD OF TURIN

One of Turin's most well-known religious relics is the **Shroud of Turin**, a centuries-old linen cloth that some people believe to depict the image of Jesus Christ. While it draws many visitors for its historical and religious significance, focusing solely on the Shroud can lead you to miss much of what this fascinating city has to offer. Moreover, the Shroud is only displayed on rare occasions, and when it's not, visitors can only see a replica in the **Cathedral of St. John the Baptist.**

WHY SHOULD YOU AVOID IT?

The Shroud of Turin, though historically significant, is not always on display. Many visitors arrive expecting to see the original Shroud but are met with a replica instead. Furthermore, if you focus your visit around the Shroud, you might overlook Turin's other incredible attractions, such as its world-class museums, grand piazzas, and unique culture. The city is full of art, history, and architectural beauty beyond just the Shroud.

It is possible to restrict your experience and miss out on Turin's greater cultural diversity if you concentrate solely on this one religious relic.

WHAT TO DO INSTEAD?

- **Explore the Museo Egizio:** After visiting the **Cathedral of St. John the Baptist,** head to the **Museo Egizio,** one of the most important Egyptian museums in the world. Its vast collection of ancient Egyptian artifacts offers an enthralling look into the past.
- **Visit the Mole Antonelliana and Cinema Museum:** The **Mole Antonelliana** is Turin's most iconic building and houses the **National Museum of Cinema**. For amazing views of the city and the Alps, take the elevator to the top.
- **Discover Turin's Royal Palaces:** Turin's royal heritage is evident in its grand palaces, such as the **Palazzo Reale** and **Palazzo Madama**. These magnificent structures are must-see sights that provide a glimpse into the city's regal past.

ADDITIONAL TIPS

- **Check Display Dates for the Shroud**: If your visit is centered around the Shroud of Turin, check in advance to see if the original will be on display. Usually, the relic is only displayed to the general public during special exhibitions.

- **Plan a Well-Rounded Itinerary**: If you want to fully appreciate Turin's beauty, make sure your trip includes a variety of religious, historical, and cultural sites.

By expanding your itinerary beyond the Shroud of Turin, you'll discover the broader cultural and historical richness of this elegant city.

2. SKIP DINING IN THE MAIN TOURIST SQUARES

Turin's beautiful squares, like **Piazza Castello** and **Piazza San Carlo**, are iconic and picturesque. However, the restaurants and cafés in these main tourist areas often cater to visitors with higher prices and less authentic food. If you eat at these places, you might have to pay more for a meal that doesn't accurately represent the well-known cuisine of the area.

WHY SHOULD YOU AVOID IT?

- Restaurants and cafés in the main squares tend to be overpriced, offering menus that are often simplified for tourists. You might miss out on the true flavors of Piedmontese cuisine, such as **vitello tonnato, bagna càuda**, or **agnolotti**, if you stick to eateries in heavily touristed areas. In addition, the atmosphere in these bustling squares sometimes seems more impersonal and hurried than in the more cozy neighborhood trattorias where residents eat.

These tourist-oriented spots may lack the authenticity and quality you'll find in the smaller, less central restaurants scattered throughout Turin.

WHAT TO DO INSTEAD?

- **Explore Neighborhood Trattorias:** Step away from the main squares and venture into quieter neighborhoods like **San Salvario** or **Vanchiglia**, where you'll find family-run trattorias offering authentic Piedmontese dishes at much more reasonable prices. These locations provide authentically prepared, traditionally-served local cuisine.
- **Dine in the Quadrilatero Romano District:** The **Quadrilatero Romano**

is known for its excellent dining options and is popular with locals. Away from the throngs of tourists, the narrow streets are home to quaint osterias and contemporary eateries serving some of Turin's best food.

- **: Look for Traditional Piedmontese Cuisine:** When choosing a restaurant, look for menus that include local specialties like **tajarin** (thin egg pasta), **bollito misto** (mixed boiled meats), and **Piedmontese wines** like **Barolo** and **Barbera**. These are frequently indicators that the restaurant you're visiting takes pleasure in providing real regional cuisine.

ADDITIONAL TIPS

- **Check Reviews**: Before choosing a place to eat, check online reviews from locals to get a sense of the quality and authenticity of the food.
- **Avoid "Tourist Menus"**: Be cautious of restaurants that offer multi-language menus and tourist set menus, as these places tend to focus on volume over quality.

By avoiding the touristy restaurants in Turin's main squares and seeking out local, off-the-beaten-path dining spots, you'll have a more genuine and unforgettable eating experience.

3. DON'T IGNORE TURIN'S APERITIVO CULTURE

Turin is the birthplace of the **aperitivo**, the beloved Italian tradition of enjoying pre-dinner drinks accompanied by a generous spread of snacks. One of the nicest parts of Turin's local culture will be lost if you miss this ritual. The city takes aperitivo seriously, and it's much more than just a casual drink before dinner—it's a social experience, often with an abundance of delicious food.

WHY SHOULD YOU AVOID IT?

- Skipping aperitivo in Turin means missing out on a key part of the city's social life and culinary culture. While some tourists may associate aperitivo with simply enjoying a quick drink, in Turin it refers to the chance to indulge in a spread of snacks or buffet that frequently rivals a full meal. Aperitivo spots offer everything from local cheeses, cured meats, and small sandwiches to pasta, salads, and savory pastries. Plus, enjoying a drink like **Vermouth di Torino** or a classic **Negroni** in one of the city's historic cafés allows you to experience a more authentic side of Turin.

By not participating in this ritual, you may miss out on an excellent (and affordable) way to dine, particularly if you're on a tight budget.

WHAT TO DO INSTEAD?

- **Enjoy Aperitivo in Historic Cafés**: Turin is home to some of Italy's oldest and most beautiful cafés, such as **Caffè Torino** and **Caffè Mulassano**. These elegant spots serve up classic aperitivo drinks alongside delicious snacks. Sip on a traditional **Vermouth di Torino** or **Campari**, both local specialties, while soaking in the café's old-world charm.
- **Try Modern Aperitivo Bars**: For a more contemporary take on aperitivo, head to bars in neighborhoods like **San Salvario** or **Quadrilatero Romano**, where you'll find hip spots serving craft cocktails and more creative snack spreads. This tradition's contemporary interpretation combines Turin's changing culinary scene with its historical origins.
- **Opt for Vermouth-Based Cocktails**: Vermouth originated in Turin, and a lot of aperitivo bars will have a selection of drinks made with vermouth. Whether you choose a **Negroni**, a **Vermouth Tonic**, or a simple glass of vermouth on the rocks, it's the perfect way to experience this local tradition.

ADDITIONAL TIPS

- **Plan Aperitivo Before Dinner**: Aperitivo in Turin is typically served between 6:00 and 8:00 PM. It's a great way to start the evening before going out to a late dinner, or if the spread is large enough, it can even take the place of dinner entirely.
- **Look for Apericena**: Some bars in Turin offer **apericena**, a combination of aperitivo and cena (dinner), where the food offered is hearty enough to replace a full meal.

By embracing Turin's aperitivo culture, you'll experience one of the city's most enjoyable traditions, combining socializing with delicious food and drinks.

4. AVOID RUSHING THROUGH THE EGYPTIAN MUSEUM

The **Museo Egizio** in Turin is the second-largest Egyptian museum in the world, boasting an extraordinary collection of artifacts that span over 5,000 years of history. Many travelers, eager to see multiple attractions in one day, make the mistake of rushing through this museum. They lose out on completely understanding the breadth and importance of its exhibits if they do this.

WHY SHOULD YOU AVOID IT?

- The **Museo Egizio** is home to over 30,000 artifacts, including mummies, statues, papyri, and tomb treasures, making it one of Turin's top cultural attractions. However, due to its vastness, it's easy to feel overwhelmed if you rush through it. Skimming through exhibits will rob you of the opportunity to truly engage with the fascinating history of Ancient Egypt and the incredible preservation of these artifacts. The importance of the museum is found in the intricate narratives that accompany the large-scale exhibits.

A rushed visit may leave you feeling like you haven't absorbed much, especially given the size of the museum and the sheer number of exhibits. To make the most of your time here, it's essential to take a slower pace and focus on key pieces.

WHAT TO DO INSTEAD?

- **Plan for a Longer Visit:** Allocate a minimum of several hours to thoroughly investigate the museum. Take your time to read the information accompanying the exhibits, and don't hesitate to use the audio guide or museum app to gain more in-depth insights into the artifacts.
- **Join a Guided Tour:** Take into account signing up for a guided tour of the

museum. A knowledgeable guide can provide a deeper understanding of the artifacts and their historical context, making your visit more meaningful. Guided tours also help you focus on the museum's most significant pieces without feeling overwhelmed by the vast collection.

- **Focus on Highlights:** If you have limited time, focus on the museum's main highlights, such as the **Tomb of Kha and Merit**, the **Statue of Ramses II**, and the museum's incredible collection of **papyrus manuscripts**. These important displays provide you with a closer understanding of the history of Ancient Egypt while demonstrating the collection's richness.

ADDITIONAL TIPS

- **Visit During Off-Peak Hours**: to have a more laid-back experience and stay away from crowds, visit the Museo Egizio early in the morning or later in the afternoon.
- **Take Breaks**: The museum is large, so don't hesitate to take short breaks between exhibits. The museum café offers a perfect spot to relax and recharge before continuing your exploration.

By taking the time to fully explore the Museo Egizio, you'll gain a deeper appreciation of Ancient Egyptian history and Turin's important role in preserving these cultural treasures.

5. DON'T DRIVE IN THE HISTORIC CENTER

The historic center of Turin is a lovely place with opulent streets, expansive piazzas, and important historical sites, but driving through it can be quite difficult. Many visitors make the mistake of driving in the city center, only to find themselves facing restricted access zones, limited parking, and heavy traffic. Turin's **ZTL** (Zona a Traffico Limitato) restricts car access in many parts of the city center, making it not only difficult but costly for tourists unfamiliar with the system.

WHY SHOULD YOU AVOID IT?

- The **ZTL** (limited traffic zones) in Turin's historic center are strictly enforced, with hefty fines for unauthorized vehicles entering restricted areas. These zones are designed to reduce traffic congestion and pollution, and they apply during specific hours. Many tourists unknowingly drive into these areas, thinking they are open to general traffic, only to receive fines by mail after their visit. In addition to being hard to come by, parking in the city center is frequently pricy.

Additionally, Turin is a walkable city with an excellent public transportation system. Driving not only complicates your visit but also deprives you of the chance to enjoy the city's charm on foot or by tram.

WHAT TO DO INSTEAD?

- **Use Public Transportation:** Without a car, getting around Turin is simple thanks to the city's effective public transportation system, which consists of buses, metro lines, and trams. The **GTT** (Gruppo Torinese Trasporti) operates the city's transport network, and tickets are available for purchase at most newsstands and metro stations. Opt for trams, which provide a scenic and relaxing way to explore the city.
- **Walk Through the Historic Center:** Walking through Turin's historic center is the best way to experience it. The city's grid-like layout makes it easy to navigate, and walking allows you to take in the architecture, explore hidden alleys, and visit cafés and shops at your own pace. Turin's elegant arcades also provide shelter from rain or sun, making walking pleasant in any weather.
- **Rent a Bike:** Turin is also a bike-friendly city, with bike rental services and designated bike lanes throughout the center. Renting a bike allows you to cover more ground while enjoying the city at a leisurely pace. Additionally, you won't have to deal with the headache of parking or traffic.

ADDITIONAL TIPS

- **Check ZTL Hours:** If you absolutely need to drive, make sure you're aware of the ZTL hours and restricted areas to avoid fines. Maps and schedules are available at local tourist information centers or on the city's website.
- **Park Outside the Center:** If you must drive into Turin, consider parking in one of the city's outskirts or designated parking lots and then take public transportation into the center.

By avoiding driving in Turin's historic center and opting for public transport, walking, or cycling, you'll enjoy a stress-free and more immersive experience of the city.

6. DON'T SKIP THE QUADRILATERO ROMANO DISTRICT

One of Turin's oldest and liveliest neighborhoods is the **Quadrilatero Romano**, which is home to chic bars, traditional eateries, old buildings, and small, winding streets. Many tourists focus on the more famous landmarks like the **Mole Antonelliana** and **Piazza Castello**, overlooking this area. Skipping the **Quadrilatero Romano** means missing out on a unique part of Turin where modern life blends with ancient history.

WHY SHOULD YOU AVOID IT?

- The **Quadrilatero Romano** is a lively and diverse area, home to some of the best dining and nightlife in the city. It's a great place to experience Turin's local atmosphere, far from the more tourist-heavy areas. This neighborhood, which dates back to the Roman era, is also full of historical sites, including stunning churches, secret courtyards, and lively piazzas.
- If you stick to only the main tourist spots and skip this district, you'll miss the chance to explore the heart of Turin's local life. The **Quadrilatero Romano** offers a more intimate and authentic glimpse of the city, with small boutiques, artisan shops, and cozy cafés.

WHAT TO DO INSTEAD?

- **Explore the Neighborhood's Nightlife:** The **Quadrilatero Romano** comes alive in the evening, with bustling bars and restaurants offering aperitivo and dinner. This is the place to be if you want to take in Turin's lively nightlife or just relax with a glass of wine. Look for local spots where you can savor authentic **Piedmontese** dishes paired with regional wines.
- **Visit the Area's Historical Sites:** One of Italy's best-preserved Roman gates, the **Palatine Towers**, is one of the district's many significant historical landmarks. You'll also find the stunning **Santuario della Consolata**, a beautiful Baroque church that's well worth a visit.
- **Wander Through Local Markets and Shops:** During the day, the streets of the **Quadrilatero Romano** are filled with small artisan shops and boutiques. The nearby **Porta Palazzo Market** is the largest open-air market in Europe and a great place to find fresh produce, local cheeses, and regional specialties.

ADDITIONAL TIPS

- **Enjoy Aperitivo Here:** The **Quadrilatero Romano** is an excellent area to enjoy aperitivo in the evening. Many bars serve generous spreads of local delicacies, allowing you to taste a variety of Piedmontese snacks.
- **Visit During Both Day and Night:** The district has a different feel depending on the time of day. Visit it during the day for sightseeing and shopping, then come back for dinner or drinks in the evening.
- By including the **Quadrilatero Romano** in your Turin itinerary, you'll experience the city's rich history and vibrant local culture, all within one of its most dynamic neighborhoods.

7. DON'T SKIP A VISIT TO MOLE ANTONELLIANA

The **Mole Antonelliana** is one of Turin's most iconic landmarks, and while many tourists may be tempted to admire it from the outside, skipping the interior and its unique attractions would be a missed opportunity. The **Mole,** originally conceived as a synagogue, now houses the **National Museum of Cinema**, one of the best museums in the world dedicated to the history of film. With the surrounding Alps framing the city, the panoramic views from the top provide one of the best vantage points to see the entirety of Turin beyond the exhibits.

WHY SHOULD YOU AVOID IT?

- The **Mole Antonelliana** is not just a striking piece of architecture; it offers a deeply immersive experience into both Italian and international cinema. If you simply admire it from the outside, you'll miss the fascinating exhibits inside the **National Museum of Cinema**, which trace the history of filmmaking through interactive displays, rare artifacts, and multimedia installations. The museum itself has a breathtaking interior that provides for a truly unique cinematic experience.
- Additionally, visitors can take a glass elevator to the top of the **Mole** for breathtaking 360-degree views of the city and the Alps beyond. Ignoring this experience would be like missing one of Turin's most memorable attractions.

WHAT TO DO INSTEAD?

- **Explore the National Museum of Cinema:** Dive into the world of cinema by exploring the **National Museum of Cinema** housed within the **Mole Antonelliana**. The museum takes visitors on a journey through the history of film, with a wide range of exhibits, from early silent films to modern cinema. Cinema enthusiasts will particularly value the unique collections and movie memorabilia.
- **Take the Elevator to the Top:** One of the best parts of visiting the **Mole Antonelliana** is the glass elevator ride to the top. The panoramic terrace offers stunning views of Turin's skyline, framed by the **Alps** in the distance. You shouldn't miss the highlight, which is the view from the top, whether you go there during the day or at night.
- **Learn About the Mole's History:** While visiting, take time to learn about

the fascinating history of the **Mole Antonelliana**, originally designed as a synagogue and now a symbol of Turin. Its historical, cultural changes and architectural significance give your visit more depth.

ADDITIONAL TIPS

- **Book Tickets in Advance**: The **Mole Antonelliana** is one of Turin's most popular attractions, so booking tickets ahead of time can save you from long lines, especially for the elevator to the top.
- **Visit During Different Times of Day**: Depending on the time of day, the top views vary, so consider visiting in the morning for clearer views of the Alps, or later in the afternoon for a beautiful sunset over the city.
- By making time to visit the **Mole Antonelliana** and exploring its interior, you'll not only enjoy one of Turin's best museums but also gain a unique perspective of the city's skyline from its highest point.

8. AVOID VISITING ONLY IN WINTER

While Turin's proximity to the **Alps** makes it a popular winter destination for skiing and snow sports, visiting the city exclusively in winter means missing out on some of its most vibrant and beautiful seasons. Turin shines in the spring and fall when outdoor activities, festivals, and events are in full swing, but winter has its own charm as well, with the city decked out in festive lights and crowds drawn to the nearby ski resorts.

WHY SHOULD YOU AVOID IT?

Winter in Turin can be cold, and while the city has its appeal during the holiday season, with cozy cafés and Christmas markets, it may limit your ability to enjoy some of the best outdoor experiences the city has to offer. Winter can bring shorter days and fewer outdoor events, but warmer weather is ideal for enjoying many of Turin's beautiful parks and outdoor cafés.

- With milder temperatures, Turin comes alive in the spring and fall when the city organizes a number of culinary and cultural events. The blooming gardens of **Parco del Valentino** and the vibrant **Piazza Castello** make these seasons particularly attractive for visitors. Moreover, fall is the perfect time to explore the Piedmont region's world-class vineyards and indulge in local food festivals.

WHAT TO DO INSTEAD?

- **Visit in Spring for Blooming Gardens:** Warm weather in the springtime makes Turin ideal for exploring its parks, going to outdoor markets, and taking advantage of the city's outdoor cafés. The **Parco del Valentino** is especially beautiful in spring, with blooming flowers and riverside walks that make for a peaceful escape.
- **Explore Turin's Festivals in the Fall:** Fall in Turin is rich with events and festivals. The **Salone del Gusto**, an international food fair, takes place in October, offering visitors a chance to experience the best of local and international cuisine. You can enjoy vineyard tours and wine tastings in the nearby **Langhe** wine region during the fall, which is also a great time to visit.
- **Enjoy Turin's Aperitivo Outdoors:** Enjoying Turin's renowned aperitivo culture is best done in the spring or fall on outdoor terraces. Bars across the city offer generous aperitivo spreads, and sitting outside on a warm evening is the perfect way to experience Turin's social scene.

ADDITIONAL TIPS

- **Plan Around Events:** Check the local event calendar before your visit. Turin is home to several major festivals throughout the year, particularly in spring and fall, which can add to your cultural experience.
- **Explore the Piedmont Countryside:** Use the mild weather to explore the surrounding Piedmont region, famous for its wine, truffles, and charming villages.

By visiting Turin during spring or fall, you'll experience the city at its best, with more outdoor activities, festivals, and a lively atmosphere that's harder to enjoy in winter's colder months.

9. DON'T MISS THE PALATINE TOWERS

The **Palatine Towers** (**Porte Palatine**) are one of the most well-preserved Roman gates in the world, dating back to the 1st century BC. While many visitors to Turin focus on more modern landmarks like the **Mole Antonelliana** or the **Royal Palace**, skipping the **Palatine Towers** means missing out on a significant part of Turin's ancient history. Anyone interested in the Roman history of the city must visit this landmark.

WHY SHOULD YOU AVOID IT?

- The **Palatine Towers** offer a unique glimpse into Turin's Roman origins. The twin towers, along with the adjacent Roman wall, are some of the best-preserved remnants of Roman architecture in northern Italy. Skipping this site means missing out on an opportunity to see one of Turin's most ancient and historically significant landmarks, which provides a direct link to the city's roots as a Roman settlement known as **Augusta Taurinorum**.
- The quiet surroundings of the towers provide a respite from the bustling city and let guests appreciate the historical significance of this old gate. It's also located near other key attractions, such as the **Cathedral of San Giovanni Battista**, making it easy to include in your itinerary.

WHAT TO DO INSTEAD?

- **Explore the Palatine Towers:** Spend time walking around the **Palatine Towers** to admire their impressive structure and learn about their significance in Turin's Roman past. Going through the old gate offers you an idea of the city's lengthy history. The towers were originally the main entrance to the Roman city.
- **Visit the Archaeological Park:** The **Palatine Towers** are part of an archaeological park that also includes Roman ruins and ancient remains of the city's walls. The park is a serene, picturesque location where you can unwind and enjoy the layers of Turin's history without having to go to the busier parts of the city.

- **Combine with a Visit to Turin Cathedral:** Just a short walk from the **Palatine Towers** is the **Cathedral of San Giovanni Battista**, which houses the **Shroud of Turin**. Turin's religious importance and Roman past come together beautifully when combined with a visit to the towers.

ADDITIONAL TIPS

- **Visit Early:** The **Palatine Towers** are best visited early in the day when the site is quieter and you can fully appreciate the ancient architecture without the crowds.
- **Take a Walking Tour:** Consider joining a guided walking tour that includes the **Palatine Towers** as part of a broader exploration of Turin's historical landmarks.
- By making time to visit the **Palatine Towers**, you'll gain a deeper understanding of Turin's rich Roman history and experience a quieter, often overlooked, part of the city's cultural heritage.

10. AVOID UNDERESTIMATING TURIN'S COFFEE CULTURE

Coffee has a long and illustrious history in Turin, and to avoid it would be to miss out on a fundamental aspect of the local way of life. Turin is home to some of Italy's oldest and most elegant cafés, where enjoying a cup of coffee is not just a quick stop but a deeply ingrained social and cultural experience. If you underestimate this tradition by opting for a quick chain coffee or not stopping for a proper café visit, you'll miss a rich part of Turin's history.

WHY SHOULD YOU AVOID IT?

There is a distinct coffee culture in Turin compared to other regions of Italy. Here, people usually sit down to enjoy their coffee, which is usually paired with small pastries or chocolates, rather than just grabbing a quick espresso at the counter. Skipping this experience or choosing a chain café over one of Turin's historic coffeehouses would mean missing out on the ritual that has defined the city's social scene for centuries.

- One of Turin's specialties is the **bickering**, a layered drink made with espresso, chocolate, and cream, which originated in the city's historic cafés. Missing this drink and the atmosphere of the ornate, old-world cafés is skipping a key part of Turin's charm.

WHAT TO DO INSTEAD?

- **Visit Historic Cafés:** Turin is known for its grand historic cafés, such as **Caffè Torino, Caffè Mulassano,** and **Baratti & Milano**, which have been serving locals and visitors for centuries. In addition to having excellent coffee, these cafés are renowned for their tasteful interiors, which offer a sophisticated, vintage ambiance in which to sit and enjoy a drink.
- **Try the Bicerin:** One of Turin's signature drinks is the **bickering**, a luxurious combination of coffee, chocolate, and cream. Make sure to try this drink at **Caffè Al Bicerin**, the café where it was invented. It's the ideal way to get a taste of a special aspect of the city's coffee culture.
- **Pair Your Coffee with Local Pastries:** Don't just settle for an espresso—pair your coffee with a **gianduiotto**, a local chocolate made with hazelnuts, or other regional pastries. Cafés in Turin are renowned for their wide selection of sweets, which elevate the coffee-drinking experience.

ADDITIONAL TIPS

- **Take Your Time:** Don't rush your coffee break. Turin's café culture is about slowing down, enjoying your drink, and soaking in the atmosphere, so take your time to sit and relax.
- **Avoid Chain Coffee Shops:** Skip international coffee chains in favor of Turin's local establishments. You'll get better quality coffee and a more authentic experience.

By embracing Turin's coffee culture and making time to visit its historic cafés, you'll experience a cherished tradition that reflects the city's rich history and refined lifestyle.

Turin offers a distinctive fusion of old-world charm and contemporary Italian living thanks to its rich history, beautiful architecture, and lively cultural traditions. While the city is filled with remarkable landmarks, world-class museums, and exquisite cuisine, knowing what to avoid can help you make the most of your visit. From steering clear of tourist traps to embracing local traditions like aperitivo and the city's renowned coffee culture, navigating Turin thoughtfully will ensure a more enriching and authentic experience.

By exploring beyond the usual highlights, such as the **Leaning Tower** or touristy restaurants, and instead immersing yourself in hidden gems like the **Quadrilatero Romano**, or visiting historic sites like the **Palatine Towers**, you'll discover a deeper layer of Turin that many tourists miss. Piedmont's vibrant flavors can also be fully experienced by indulging in Turin's culinary delights, such as the city's rich aperitivo spreads and its renowned **bicerin**.

By following these tips and avoiding the common mistakes travelers often make, you'll leave Turin with a genuine appreciation for its culture, history, and unique Italian charm.

SIENA

Siena, a jewel in the heart of Tuscany, is a city that transports visitors back to Italy's medieval past. Known for its well-preserved Gothic architecture, winding streets, and the iconic **Piazza del Campo**, Siena offers a captivating blend of history, art, and culture. Because Siena has preserved much of its medieval charm, unlike many other Tuscan cities, exploring its winding lanes and grand squares truly feels like traveling back in time.

Famous for the biannual **Palio di Siena**, a centuries-old horse race that brings the city's 17 historic **contrade** (districts) to life, Siena is deeply rooted in tradition. These contrade aren't just neighborhoods—they represent the soul of the city and play a central role in its identity. The contrade contributes a distinctive layer of local culture that sets Siena apart from other Italian travel destinations, from their colorful flags and emblems to their fervent celebrations.

Beyond its lively traditions, Siena boasts architectural treasures like the **Siena Cathedral (Duomo)**, a masterpiece of Gothic design, and the towering **Torre del Mangia**, offering breathtaking views over the Tuscan countryside. Everyone who visits Siena is left with a lasting impression, whether they are exploring the city's rich artistic legacy, sipping wine from the neighboring Chianti region, or meandering through the medieval streets.

In this guide, we'll explore the common mistakes travelers make when visiting Siena and how to avoid them, ensuring that your time in this historic city is as rewarding and authentic as possible.

1. AVOID VISITING DURING THE PALIO WITHOUT PROPER PREPARATION

The **Palio di Siena** is one of the most famous and historic events in Italy, held twice a year in July and August. While it's an incredible experience, visiting during the Palio without adequate preparation can lead to frustration due to the huge crowds, limited access to attractions, and high costs for accommodations. Being at the Palio is a once-in-a-lifetime experience that needs careful preparation.

WHY SHOULD YOU AVOID IT?

- The **Palio di Siena** attracts thousands of visitors, and the city becomes incredibly crowded during the event. If you're not prepared, you may find it difficult to navigate the city, access popular sites like the **Duomo** or **Piazza del Campo**, or even find a place to stay. Hotels and accommodations book up months in advance, and prices skyrocket. Furthermore, standing in the middle of the piazza to view the Palio can be uncomfortable because there isn't much space or shade, and it can be exhausting if you don't know what to expect.

If you visit during the Palio without proper planning, you might miss out on fully enjoying this historic event or other parts of Siena.

WHAT TO DO INSTEAD?

- **Plan and Book in Advance:** If you want to experience the Palio, make sure to book your accommodations and event tickets far in advance. Premium spots to watch the race, such as balconies and terrace seats, sell out quickly but offer a much more comfortable view of the action. To help you navigate the Palio customs and locate the best viewing locations, think about hiring a local guide.
- **Visit Siena Outside of the Palio Season:** If you're not specifically coming for the Palio, consider visiting Siena during a quieter time. You'll have easier access to all the major attractions without the crowds, and you'll still

be able to appreciate the city's charm and beauty. The contrade is still in place throughout the year, and you can find out more about the significance of the Palio by visiting their museums.

ADDITIONAL TIPS

- **Know the Palio Schedule**: The Palio events span several days, including processions and trials before the race. Plan to attend these in addition to race day if you want to fully immerse yourself in the experience.
- **Be Prepared for Crowds**: If you do attend the Palio, arrive early, dress for the heat, and be ready for the intense energy of the crowd, especially in the standing-room area of the Piazza del Campo.

By properly preparing for the Palio, you can fully enjoy this extraordinary event and avoid the pitfalls that come with the large crowds and high demand for accommodations.

2. SKIP EATING AT RESTAURANTS IN PIAZZA DEL CAMPO

The **Piazza del Campo** is the heart of Siena and one of Italy's most stunning squares, famous for its fan-shaped design and for hosting the **Palio di Siena**. Although it's a fantastic location, the eateries right in the square are usually overpriced, serve mostly tourists, and frequently serve subpar food at exorbitant costs.

WHY SHOULD YOU AVOID IT?

- Restaurants in **Piazza del Campo** charge a premium for their location. While the view of the square is undoubtedly beautiful, the quality of the food often doesn't match the price. Many of these establishments serve generic, tourist-oriented dishes that lack the authenticity of true Tuscan cuisine. In comparison to other parts of the city, you will probably pay more for a meal here, and you will also be missing out on more genuine dining experiences that are available a short distance away.
- Additionally, these restaurants tend to be crowded, especially during peak tourist seasons or around the time of the **Palio**, which can make for a less

enjoyable dining experience.

WHAT TO DO INSTEAD?

- **Explore Side Streets for Authentic Trattorias:** There are real Tuscan trattorias and osterias that provide a far more genuine dining experience just a short stroll from the main square. Look for places where the locals eat—these restaurants serve traditional Sienese dishes like **pici pasta**, **ribollita**, and **wild boar ragù** at much more reasonable prices.
- **Dine at Neighborhood Restaurants:** Venture into neighborhoods like **San Domenico** or **Onda** for some of the best local cuisine. These areas have smaller, family-run restaurants where the focus is on quality and tradition. You'll experience a more laid-back vibe and gain a deeper understanding of the city's culinary legacy.
- **Try Aperitivo Instead:** If you want to enjoy the beauty of **Piazza del Campo** without the hefty restaurant bill, consider having a drink at one of the cafés around the square during aperitivo hour. Without spending a lot of money on a meal, you can enjoy a glass of the region's wine or a **spritz** while admiring the scenery.

ADDITIONAL TIPS

- **Check Reviews:** Before choosing a place to eat, look for online reviews or ask locals for recommendations to find the best dining spots that offer authentic Tuscan cuisine.
- **Avoid Tourist Menus:** Restaurants with menus in multiple languages and tourist set menus often focus on quantity over quality. Opt for places that offer traditional Tuscan dishes and seasonal ingredients.
- By skipping the restaurants in **Piazza del Campo** and venturing into Siena's side streets and neighborhoods, you'll enjoy more authentic and flavorful meals at a much better value.

3. AVOID CLIMBING THE TORRE DEL MANGIA AT MIDDAY

The **Torre del Mangia,** located in **Piazza del Campo,** offers stunning panoramic views of Siena and the surrounding Tuscan countryside. While visiting the tower in the middle of the day is a must, doing so in the summer can result in uncomfortable crowds, long lines, and crowded conditions.

WHY SHOULD YOU AVOID IT?

- The narrow staircase of the **Torre del Mangia** can become quite crowded during peak tourist hours, making the climb feel cramped and uncomfortable. In addition, climbing over 400 steps in the midday sun can be exhausting, especially in the heat of the summer months. During these hours, it may also get crowded on the top viewing platform, making it harder to take in the entire view.

The heat inside the tower and the lengthy waits in the sun before the climb can detract from the experience. If you're visiting Siena in the summer, midday climbs can be particularly draining and might leave you feeling rushed.

WHAT TO DO INSTEAD?

- **Visit Early in the Morning or Late in the Afternoon:** Plan to climb the **Torre del Mangia** either early in the morning, right when it opens, or later in the afternoon. These times tend to be less crowded, and the temperatures are much more comfortable, especially in the warmer months. The Tuscan countryside is bathed in morning or evening sunlight during these hours, adding to the breathtaking views due to the softer light.
- **Take Your Time to Enjoy the Views:** When you reach the top, take your time to fully appreciate the 360-degree views of Siena and the surrounding landscape. When you're not battling through crowds or hurrying through the experience because it's hot or uncomfortable, you'll enjoy it much more.
- **Combine with a Visit to the Palazzo Pubblico:** The **Torre del Mangia** is

part of the **Palazzo Pubblico**, which houses the **Civic Museum**. After climbing the tower, take some time to explore this beautiful museum, which includes famous frescoes like **Ambrogio Lorenzetti's Allegory of Good and Bad Government**.

ADDITIONAL TIPS

- **Check Opening Times**: Make sure to check the tower's opening hours ahead of time, as they can vary depending on the season.
- **Wear Comfortable Shoes**: The climb is steep and requires a good amount of energy, so wear comfortable shoes that provide support for the ascent.
- By choosing to climb the **Torre del Mangia** at off-peak times and avoiding the midday heat, you'll experience less crowds, breathtaking views, and a more satisfying and comfortable experience.

4. DON'T RELY SOLELY ON PUBLIC TRANSPORTATION

The best way to explore Siena's historic center on foot is through its compact, pedestrian-friendly city. While public transportation is available and useful for reaching the outskirts or nearby towns, relying solely on buses or taxis can prevent you from fully experiencing the beauty and charm of Siena's narrow streets, hidden alleyways, and medieval architecture.

WHY SHOULD YOU AVOID IT?

- Siena's narrow, winding streets are often inaccessible by public transportation, and buses can only take you to certain parts of the city. Many of Siena's most charming areas, like the **Piazza del Campo**, **Siena Cathedral**, and its picturesque side streets, are best explored by walking. Over-reliance on public transportation may prevent you from fully experiencing Siena's distinct personality and undiscovered attractions. Additionally, buses and taxis may not be as frequent or available as you might expect, especially in the evening.

Siena is built on a series of hills, and walking its streets allows you to appreciate its layout and the stunning views that appear at every corner. If you stick to using transportation, you may miss these subtle yet important aspects of the city.

WHAT TO DO INSTEAD?

- **Walk Through the Historic Center:** Siena's historic center is a UNESCO World Heritage site and is designed to be walked. From the **Piazza del Campo** to the **Duomo**, the best way to experience the city is by foot. Strolling around the Tuscan countryside allows you to experience the atmosphere of the Middle Ages, find charming cafés and shops, and come across breathtaking vistas.
- **Use Public Transport for Longer Distances:** Public transportation is still useful for getting to destinations outside the city center, such as the **Basilica of San Domenico** or the nearby hill towns of Tuscany. For longer travels, take the bus; however, once you're inside the city limits, use your feet to explore.
- **Wear Comfortable Shoes:** Siena's hilly terrain and cobblestone streets can be tough on your feet, so make sure to wear comfortable shoes that provide support for walking. You can easily and comfortably explore the city if you wear the appropriate shoes.

ADDITIONAL TIPS

- **Plan Walking Routes:** While walking through Siena's streets, plan routes that take you through major landmarks as well as quieter areas to get the full experience.
- **Take Breaks at Local Cafés:** Walking all day can be tiring, so be sure to stop at a local café or trattoria to rest and recharge with a coffee or a glass of Tuscan wine.

By relying on walking and using public transportation only when necessary, you'll get a more immersive and authentic experience of Siena's medieval charm.

5. AVOID RUSHING THROUGH THE SIENA CATHEDRAL (DUOMO)

The **Siena Cathedral (Duomo)** is one of the most magnificent Gothic churches in Italy, with its stunning façade, intricate interiors, and world-class artworks. It is a common mistake for tourists to rush through this architectural wonder, failing to fully appreciate its artistic treasures and rich history.

WHY SHOULD YOU AVOID IT?

- The **Siena Cathedral** is not just another church; it's a treasure trove of art and history. Its elaborate floor mosaics, which are regarded as some of the most beautiful in the world, are something not to be missed if you hurry through. The cathedral also houses sculptures by **Michelangelo, Donatello,** and **Bernini,** as well as the stunning **Piccolomini Library,** which contains beautifully preserved frescoes. If you hurry through the Duomo, you might also overlook the **Crypt** and the **Baptistery**, both of which are integral parts of the cathedral complex.

By rushing your visit, you'll miss the opportunity to take in the cathedral's awe-inspiring details, from its marble floors to the dazzling colors of the stained-glass windows. In this place, you can discover countless layers of beauty and history by taking your time.

WHAT TO DO INSTEAD?

- **Purchase the OPA SI Pass:** The **OPA SI Pass** grants access to the entire cathedral complex, including the **Piccolomini Library, Crypt, Baptistery,** and **Museo dell'Opera del Duomo**. With this pass, you can take your time exploring each section without feeling rushed.
- **Take Time to Admire the Floor Mosaics:** The cathedral's marble floor mosaics are intricate and filled with symbolic detail. These mosaics are frequently covered to preserve them, but there are times of the year when they are completely unveiled and available for public viewing. Plan your visit to coincide with this, and take time to appreciate the craftsmanship

and stories behind the designs.
- **Climb the Facciatone:** For panoramic views of Siena and the surrounding Tuscan hills, climb the **Facciatone**, part of the unfinished expansion of the cathedral. The view from the top is breathtaking and well worth the effort.

ADDITIONAL TIPS

- **Use an Audio Guide or Join a Tour**: To fully appreciate the history and art within the cathedral, consider using an audio guide or joining a guided tour. This will help you understand the significance of the architecture and artwork on a deeper level.
- **Visit During Off-Peak Hours**: The Duomo can get crowded during peak tourist times. You can explore the cathedral in a more sedate and tranquil setting if you go early in the morning or later in the afternoon.
- By taking your time to explore the **Siena Cathedral** in depth, you'll have a more enriching experience, gaining a greater appreciation for its artistic and historical significance.

6. DON'T MISS EXPLORING SIENA'S CONTRADE NEIGHBORHOODS

The districts, or **contrade**, of Siena are well-known and are essential to both the city's culture and the **Palio di Siena** horse race. Each contrada has its own history, traditions, and emblem, but many tourists overlook these neighborhoods, focusing only on the main attractions like the **Piazza del Campo** and the **Duomo**.

WHY SHOULD YOU AVOID IT?

The contrade offer a deeper insight into Sienese life and culture. Each neighborhood is a close-knit community, complete with its own colors, animal emblem, and patron saint. Exploring these areas allows you to see Siena beyond its tourist sites and experience its authentic charm. Every contrada is a flurry of colorful celebrations and decorations during the Palio season, offering a window into the city's deep sense of pride and tradition.

By sticking only to the main tourist routes, you'll miss out on this unique cultural aspect of Siena, which is central to its identity and spirit.

WHAT TO DO INSTEAD?

- **Explore the Contrade on Foot:** Take time to wander through the smaller streets of Siena's different contrade. Look for the flags and emblems that mark each neighborhood, and don't hesitate to stop by local cafés or shops to engage with the locals. Every contrada has a distinct sense of community and provides a closer-knit perspective of the city.
- **Visit During the Palio Season:** If you're in Siena during the Palio, exploring the contrade is even more rewarding. Each neighborhood has its own unique celebrations, and the pride of each contrada is on full display. Many contrades have small museums where you can learn about their history and see their Palio victories displayed, even if they are not racing.

ADDITIONAL TIPS

- **Visit Contrada Museums:** Some of Siena's contrade have small museums that showcase their history, Palio victories, and unique traditions. These museums offer a fascinating look at the deep-rooted local culture.
- **Walk Away from Tourist Crowds:** Moving beyond the tourist-heavy areas will give you a better sense of the city's authentic rhythm and allow you to enjoy the quieter, picturesque streets of the contrade.

By exploring Siena's contrade neighborhoods, you'll gain a deeper understanding of the city's cultural identity and enjoy a more authentic Sienese experience.

7. DON'T VISIT ONLY FOR THE DAY

While Siena is often treated as a day-trip destination from **Florence** or other parts of Tuscany, limiting your visit to just a few hours doesn't do justice to this remarkable city. Many visitors rush in, see the main sights like **Piazza del Campo** and the **Siena Cathedral**, and then leave without experiencing the true rhythm and charm of Siena, especially after the day-trippers have gone.

WHY SHOULD YOU AVOID IT?

Siena is a city that deserves more than a few hours. If you plan on staying in the city just for the day, you will not be able to experience the more intimate and calm atmosphere that emerges in the evenings when the crowds start to thin out. Staying overnight gives you the opportunity to enjoy the city's hidden corners, peaceful streets, and local culture without the pressure of fitting everything into a short time frame. Siena's beauty isn't just in its major landmarks—it's in its medieval streets, small cafés, and the way the light hits the Tuscan hills at sunset.

- Additionally, day trips often mean rushing through the main attractions, leaving little time to savor local cuisine, explore the **contrade** neighborhoods, or take in the city's vibrant history at a slower pace. The allure of Siena lies in its capacity to transport you to a bygone era, and a more leisurely visit is the ideal way to fully enjoy this sensation.

WHAT TO DO INSTEAD?

- **Stay Overnight:** To fully enjoy Siena, plan to spend at least one night there rather than feeling compelled to see all the must-see attractions right away. The evenings in Siena are magical, as the streets quiet down and the soft lighting creates a serene atmosphere in **Piazza del Campo** and other public squares. Walking around the city in the evening or early morning offers a different, more tranquil side of Siena that most day-trippers never see.
- **Explore Beyond the Main Attractions:** With more time, you can explore Siena's lesser-known treasures, such as the **Fontebranda**, one of the city's ancient fountains, or the beautiful **San Domenico Basilica**. You'll also have the chance to wander through the **contrade**, where you can learn more about the city's unique culture and traditions, especially surrounding the **Palio**.
- **Enjoy Siena's Local Cuisine:** If you extend your stay, you can enjoy

Siena's regional cuisine at eateries that serve more locals than visitors. Enjoy **pici pasta, wild boar ragù,** or **panforte** (Siena's famous dessert) at your own pace, without feeling rushed.

ADDITIONAL TIPS

- **Visit Siena's Markets**: If you stay longer, you can experience the local market in **Piazza del Mercato**, where you'll find fresh produce, local cheeses, and handmade goods.
- **Take a Day to Explore the Countryside**: Use Siena as a base to explore nearby hill towns or vineyards in the **Chianti** or **Val d'Orcia** regions, enhancing your Tuscan experience.

By staying overnight and taking your time to explore Siena at a slower pace, you'll have a richer and more immersive experience, enabling you to fully enjoy the local customs and medieval charm of the city.

8. AVOID MISSING A VISIT TO THE MUSEO DELL'OPERA DEL DUOMO

While many visitors head straight to the **Siena Cathedral (Duomo)**, they often overlook the **Museo dell'Opera del Duomo**, an essential part of the cathedral complex that houses some of the most important works of art from Siena's history. Ignoring this museum will deprive you of a more profound comprehension of the artistic and religious legacy of the city.

WHY SHOULD YOU AVOID IT?

- The **Museo dell'Opera del Duomo** is home to several masterpieces, including **Duccio di Buoninsegna's** famous **Maestà**, a stunning altarpiece that is considered one of the greatest works of medieval art. The museum also contains beautiful sculptures, relics, and stained glass from the cathedral. Numerous items that were formerly a part of the Duomo have been relocated to the museum in order to be preserved.
- If you hurried past this museum, you would miss the opportunity to view

some of the most important works of art in Siena and to properly recognize the creative brilliance that went into building the Duomo. The museum also offers access to the **Facciatone**, a panoramic viewpoint where you can climb to the top for breathtaking views of the city and surrounding countryside.

WHAT TO DO INSTEAD?

- **Include the Museo dell'Opera in Your Cathedral Visit:** When planning your visit to the **Siena Cathedral**, make sure to include the **Museo dell'Opera del Duomo** in your itinerary. The **OPA SI Pass** grants access to the museum, the cathedral, the **Baptistery**, and other parts of the complex, so you can explore them all without missing any key sights.
- **Take Time to See Duccio's Maestà:** The **Maestà** is one of the most important works of medieval religious art, and taking the time to view it up close is a must for art lovers. The intricate panels highlight Duccio's skillful use of color and composition and depict events from the lives of Christ and the Virgin Mary.
- **Climb the Facciatone:** After exploring the museum, don't miss the opportunity to climb the **Facciatone**, the unfinished façade of the cathedral. You'll be rewarded with one of Siena's best vistas from the summit, overlooking the surrounding Tuscan hills and the city's crimson rooftops.

ADDITIONAL TIPS

- **Visit During Off-Peak Hours:** To completely appreciate the museum's assets, visit during quieter times when you can take your time to appreciate the art without the crowds.
- **Combine It with a Cathedral Tour:** Consider joining a guided tour of the **Duomo** and the museum to gain a deeper understanding of the artwork and the history of the cathedral complex.
- By including the **Museo dell'Opera del Duomo** in your visit to Siena, you'll gain a greater appreciation for the city's rich artistic legacy and enjoy

one of the best viewpoints in Tuscany.

9. DON'T EXPECT SIENA TO BE LIKE FLORENCE

While both **Siena** and **Florence** are renowned Tuscan cities, they offer very different experiences. Many travelers arrive in Siena expecting a bustling, art-filled city like Florence, but are met with Siena's more intimate, slower-paced medieval charm. If Siena doesn't live up to your expectations and you don't accept it for what it is, this comparison could leave you disappointed.

WHY SHOULD YOU AVOID IT?

- Despite being considerably smaller than Florence, Siena is more attractive due to its retention of its medieval identity than to Renaissance artwork or the opulence of Florence's palaces and museums. Florence, with its rich collection of world-famous art and bustling energy, can feel overwhelming, whereas Siena's charm comes from its narrow streets, hidden piazzas, and deep-rooted local traditions like the **Palio di Siena**.
- If you're expecting Siena to be as big as Florence, with museums and a vibrant nightlife, you may be disappointed. Siena's true beauty is in its quiet moments—walking through its winding streets, admiring the Gothic architecture of the **Duomo**, or enjoying a glass of local wine in a tranquil piazza.

WHAT TO DO INSTEAD?

- **Appreciate Siena's Medieval Atmosphere:** Embrace Siena's smaller scale and the feeling of stepping back in time. The city's well-preserved medieval architecture, narrow alleys, and historic **contrade** give you a sense of what life was like centuries ago. Walking around on foot and taking your time to discover all of Siena's hidden corners is highly recommended.
- **Focus on Siena's Unique Traditions:** Unlike Florence, which is known for its Renaissance art, Siena's identity is strongly tied to the **Palio**, its famous horse race, and the **contrade** system. Visit the museums located

within the contrade to gain insight into Siena's distinct cultural legacy and learn about the history of the city through these customs.
- **Enjoy a More Relaxed Pace:** The slower tempo of Siena is part of its charm. Take time to enjoy local dishes like **pici pasta** or **ribollita** in a family-run trattoria, or have an aperitivo in **Piazza del Campo** as the sun sets. Instead of rushing through a checklist of sights, savor the city's atmosphere.

ADDITIONAL TIPS

- **Plan for a More Intimate Experience**: While Florence dazzles with big attractions like the **Uffizi** and **David**, Siena offers a more intimate experience focused on local life, medieval history, and quiet beauty.
- **Explore the Countryside**: If you're looking for grandeur, spend a day visiting the nearby Tuscan countryside or **Chianti** wine region to see the stunning landscapes that complement Siena's charm.

By appreciating Siena for its medieval atmosphere and slower pace, you'll avoid the disappointment that comes from comparing it to Florence and instead enjoy the city's unique and tranquil beauty.

10. AVOID OVERLOOKING SIENA'S SURROUNDING COUNTRYSIDE

Many tourists to Siena never venture outside of the city's magnificent medieval architecture and historic sites, preferring to spend their time in the surrounding Tuscan countryside. While the city itself is a treasure, skipping the opportunity to explore the rolling hills, vineyards, and picturesque villages nearby means missing out on one of the region's most beautiful experiences.

WHY SHOULD YOU AVOID IT?

- One of the main things that makes people fall in love with this region of Italy is the Tuscan countryside. The landscapes around Siena, particularly in the **Val d'Orcia** and **Chianti** regions, are stunning and offer a peaceful

contrast to the city's narrow streets and bustling piazzas. By staying only within the city limits, you're missing out on the classic Tuscan experience—vineyards, olive groves, hilltop villages, and some of the best food and wine in the world.
- Many visitors regret not taking a day or two to explore the countryside, where you can enjoy wine tastings, visit charming towns like **Montepulciano** or **Montalcino**, and experience the slower, more relaxed pace of rural Tuscany.

WHAT TO DO INSTEAD?

- **Take a Day Trip to the Val d'Orcia or Chianti:** The **Val d'Orcia** is a UNESCO World Heritage site known for its picturesque landscapes, rolling hills, and cypress-lined roads. A day trip to this region allows you to visit stunning towns like **Pienza** and **San Quirico d'Orcia**. Similarly, **Chianti** is a must for wine lovers, offering vineyards, wine cellars, and beautiful villages to explore.
- **Join a Wine Tasting Tour:** Tuscany is famous for its wines, particularly **Chianti Classico** and **Brunello di Montalcino**. Joining a wine-tasting tour is a fantastic way to experience the region's rich wine culture. Along with tastings of regional wines and produce, many tours include stops at historic wine cellars, olive groves, and vineyards.
- **Visit the Hot Springs of Bagno Vignoni:** For a relaxing escape, consider visiting the thermal springs of **Bagno Vignoni**, a charming village in the Val d'Orcia. The natural hot springs are a perfect way to unwind after a day of exploring.

ADDITIONAL TIPS

- **Rent a Car for Flexibility**: To truly explore the countryside at your own pace, consider renting a car. This allows you to stop at small villages, take scenic drives, and discover hidden gems that public transportation might not reach.
- **Book a Farm Stay (Agriturismo):** Staying at an agriturismo—a working

farm that offers accommodations—is a great way to immerse yourself in rural Tuscan life. In a tranquil environment, you can savor farm-fresh meals and warm local hospitality.

By taking the time to explore the Tuscan countryside, you'll complement your visit to Siena with breathtaking scenery, world-class wine, and the authentic rural charm that makes Tuscany one of the world's most beloved regions.

Siena, with its medieval architecture, rich traditions, and vibrant local culture, offers visitors an unforgettable glimpse into Tuscany's past. However, like any popular destination, there are common pitfalls that can detract from your experience. You can experience the genuine beauty of this ancient city by avoiding tourist traps like pricey restaurants, hurrying past significant landmarks, and cutting your visit short.

From taking your time to explore the **Siena Cathedral** and delving into the city's **contrade** neighborhoods to embracing the slower pace of life and venturing into the breathtaking Tuscan countryside, Siena rewards those who are willing to move beyond the surface. No matter if you're enjoying a meal at a neighborhood trattoria, standing atop the **Torre del Mangia** at sunrise, or enjoying the sunset over the rolling hills of **Val d'Orcia**, Siena's magic, lies in its details and hidden corners.

By following these tips and giving yourself the time and space to truly explore, you'll experience a side of Siena that many visitors overlook—one that's filled with history, local charm, and a deep connection to Tuscany's cultural heritage.

FINAL REFLECTIONS

Traveling through Italy is a dream that conjures images of iconic landmarks, centuries-old art, breathtaking landscapes, and, of course, incredible cuisine. But beyond its postcard-perfect moments, Italy is also a country where tourists often find themselves caught in long lines, crowded squares, overpriced restaurants, and experiences that fall short of their expectations. This guide aims to help you travel through Italy with a more critical eye, avoiding these typical pitfalls and guiding you straight to the real heart of each place.

Throughout this book, we've explored some of Italy's most famous cities—**Rome, Venice, Florence, Turin, Siena,** and beyond—not by telling you only what to do but by shedding light on what to avoid. You learned how to get around the **Colosseum**'s long lines and where to find better restaurants away from the main tourist attractions when you were in **Rome**. In **Venice**, we explored how to sidestep the crowded gondola rides and find a more intimate, local side of the city. In **Florence**, avoiding the tourist-heavy restaurants near the **Duomo** was just as important as seeking out hidden gems in quieter neighborhoods. **Turin's** sophisticated aperitivo culture and **Siena's** contrade neighborhoods were highlighted to showcase a deeper, more local experience that many travelers overlook.

One of the most important lessons from this book is that Italy's magic isn't confined to its famous landmarks. While the **Leaning Tower of Pisa**, the **Uffizi Gallery**, and the **Colosseum** are undeniably worth visiting, Italy's true essence often lies in the moments you can't find on the usual tourist itinerary. It's in the quiet piazzas where locals congregate for an evening stroll, the tiny family-run trattorias serving recipes handed down through the generations, and the cobblestone streets of a medieval village.

You'll be able to see Italy through the eyes of the locals and avoid the tourist traps by heeding the advice in this guide. You'll know where to find the best gelato, where to enjoy a sunset without the crowds, and how to navigate each city at a slower, more thoughtful pace. Italy's diverse regions—from the rolling hills of **Tuscany** to the dramatic coastline of the **Amalfi Coast**—each offer something special, but to truly experience them, you need to look beyond the obvious and venture off the beaten path.

This book also underscores the importance of taking your time in each destination. Italy is a country to savor, not rush through. Whether you're standing before a fresco in the **Siena Cathedral**, enjoying a glass of **Chianti** in a Tuscan vineyard, or wandering the quiet streets of **Turin** after the crowds have left, it's the slower, more mindful experiences that will leave the biggest impression. You'll gain a deeper understanding and appreciation of Italy's rich history, culture, and way of life by avoiding the pitfalls of quick, superficial tourism.

In the end, Italy is a destination to fully experience using all of your senses, not just a place to visit. Whether it's tasting the freshest pasta in a hidden trattoria, hearing the echoes of ancient history in a quiet Roman ruin, or seeing the vibrant colors of the **Venetian Lagoon** at dusk, Italy's wonders reveal themselves to those who take the time to explore it thoughtfully.

Thus, as you set out on your adventure, keep in mind that the most memorable moments frequently occur when you venture off the well-traveled paths and discover your own Italian adventure. Use this guide as a tool, but also let your curiosity lead you to the hidden corners and unexpected moments that will make your trip truly unforgettable. **Buon Viaggio**, and may your Italian journey be as rich and rewarding as the country itself!

Printed in Great Britain
by Amazon